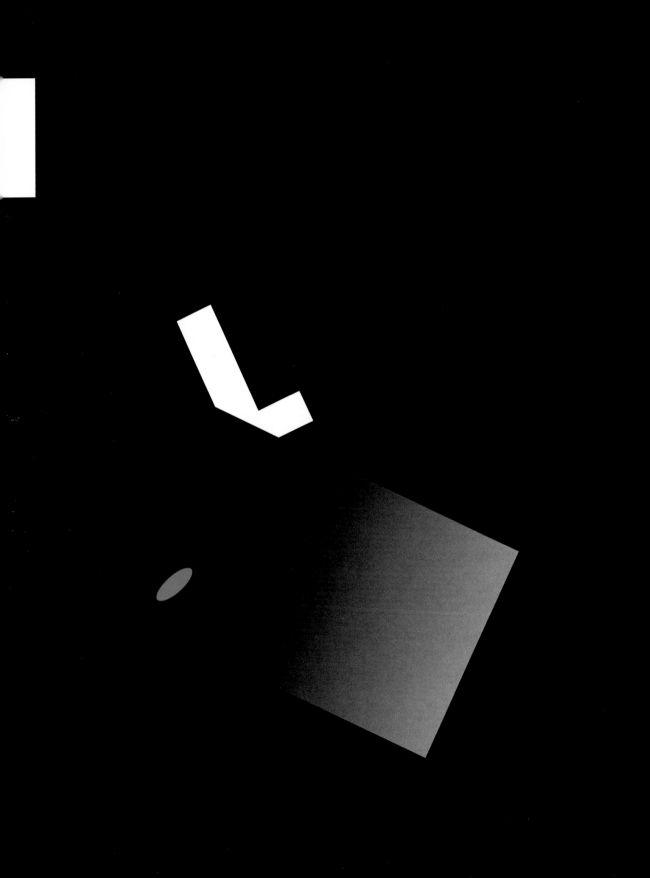

2

Working

with

Computer

Type

A RotoVision Book
Published and Distributed by RotoVision SA
Route Suisse 9
1295 Mies
Switzerland

Tel   41 (22) 775 30 55
Fax   41 (22) 755 40 72

Distributed to the trade in the United States by

Watson Guptill Publications
1515 Broadway
New York, New York 10036

ISBN 0-8230-6479-4

Book design by Rob Carter

Production and separations in Singapore by

ProVision Pte. Ltd.
Tel   65 334 7720
Fax   65 334 7721

Work with
with
Computer
Type

Rob Carter

Logotypes
Stationery Systems
Visual Identity

ROTOVISION

Introduction

to understand the inherent strengths and weaknesses of the hardware and software. Effective typographic solutions make use of the computer in just this manner.

In *Working with Computer Type 2,* you will witness a thoughtful and deliberate blending of old and new tools into a hybrid process. The computer is at its best when used in such a manner, for this is when it serves to enlighten rather than nullify the mind. In a sense, this book is a celebration of the computer, both in its design and in the case studies it presents. But more importantly, it celebrates excellent typographic design based on a sound conceptual foundation.

Perhaps the greatest obstacle hindering young designers and desktop publishers is the avoidance of the pitfalls posed by typographic tricks in software packages. Much of today's computer-generated typography seems characterized by a penetrating sameness. We may blame this lack of individuality and innovation on the elusive power of trends and fashions, and on the brooding need to conform through stylistic imitation. Now, due to the electronic workstation and the ease of generating typography, designers must practice on the firm footing of typographical principals and historic awareness.

The second in a series, this book focuses on the design of logotypes, stationery systems, and visual identity programs. Just as primitive man carved and painted images on rock walls as a way to secure a place in the world, modern individuals and business enterprizes rely on identifying marks. A logotype is an identifying mark or system of marks composed of manipulated letterforms. An identity emerges when a system is applied to all of the visual aspects of an organization. The alphabet provides the designer with a rich palette for creative exploration, while the computer offers new creative insight.

When the Macintosh big bang occurred, the graphic design and typography world was propelled onto a new path. It happened so abruptly that old guard designers scratched their heads in disbelief, marvelling at typographic tradition turned inside out. As the world as they had known it was fading in the distance, a new typographic vista came into view – rocky terrain requiring careful negotiation for safe passage. The solid ground upon which they had once stood was being challenged and redefined.

Despite the emergence of electronic publishing, the notion of change in the visual communication industry is nothing new. Historically, all major technological changes have begun in disbelief, followed by a period of resignation and adjustment and eventually full acceptance. We are now in the adjustment phase of the electronic publishing revolution, an awkward phase where perhaps the amount of bad design outweighs the good.

Some may blame the computer for the demise of typographic quality, but the real problem lies in how the computer is integrated by each individual into the design process. Faced with no other choice than to outfit their studios with computers, designers must learn to drive these machines rather than be driven by them. Each designer must take command to personalize the use of the computer and integrate it into their creative processes as appropriately and effectively as possible. A designer must know when to push the computer's off switch and pick up a pencil; one is obligated

Whether an experienced design professional, student, or fledgling desktop publisher, the case studies presented in this book will inspire ideas and creativity, help you to find an appropriate place for the computer in your own design process, and guide you in establishing a meaningful relationship with computer tools.

All of the projects presented in the book were produced, to a greater or lesser degree, with the computer. As a whole, the collection reveals a high degree of design excellence. Rather than a typical "how to" book in the use of specific design software, this volume focuses on the formal and conceptual attributes that distinguish the projects as effective typographic designs. Case studies range from flamboyant experiments to down-to-earth functional applications. Significantly, the book chronicles the design of identity programs at the gate of the 21st century.

This book is organized alphabetically by the primary typefaces used in the case studies, rather than by designer, as in the first volume. Reading the book requires active participation: descriptive captions dart in different directions, charging the pages with visual energy.

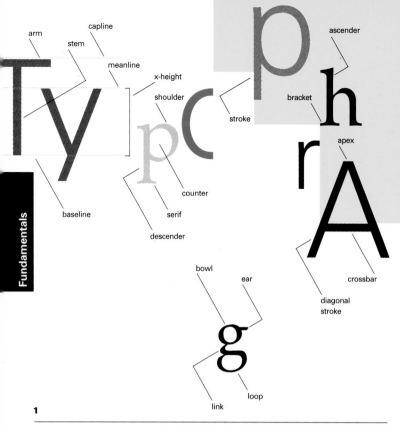

1

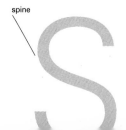

Some things never change, and in the typographic realm, principles upon which sound practice rely have remained essentially the same for centuries. These principles have over time developed in response to the way in which we read – the way in which we visually perceive the letters and words on a page. Working effectively with computer type (or working with type using any tool for that matter) requires a solid knowledge of these typographic fundamentals. The following pages provide the reader with the basic vocabulary needed for informed practice, and a fuller understanding and appreciation of the case studies presented within this book.

The anatomy of type
The colorful terms used to describe type are not unlike the terms used to describe the parts of our own bodies. Letters have arms, legs, eyes, spines, and a few other parts such as tails and stems, that we fortunately do not possess. These are the parts that have historically been used to construct letterforms. Learning this vocabulary can help the designer gain appreciation for the complexity of our alphabet, which at first glance appears very simple (fig. **1**). The structure of letters within the alphabet remains constant regardless of typeface. An uppercase *B,* for example, consists of one vertical and two curved strokes. These parts, however, may be expressed very differently from typeface to typeface (fig. **2**).

Type classification
An inexhaustible variety of type styles is available for use today, and many attempts to classify these into logical groupings have fallen short due to the overlapping visual traits of typefaces. A flawless classification system does not exist; however, a general system based on the historical development of typefaces is used widely. This delineation breaks down typefaces into the following groups: Old Style, Transitional, Modern, Slab Serif (also called Egyptian), Sans Serif, and Display (fig. **3**).

The typographic font
In desktop publishing, the terms typeface and font are often used synonymously; however, a typeface is the design of characters unified by consistent visual properties, while a font is the complete set of characters in any one design, size, or style of type. These characters include but are not limited to upper- and lower-case letters, numerals, small capitals, fractions, ligatures (two or more characters linked together into a single unit), punctuation, mathematical

B B B B B B B

2

Old Style characteristics:
Medium stroke contrast
Slanted stress
Oblique, bracketed serifs
Medium overall weight

Transitional characteristics:
Medium to high stroke contrast
Nearly vertical stress
Sharp, bracketed serifs
Slightly slanted serifs

Modern characteristics:
High stroke contrast
Vertical stress
Thin serifs
Serifs sometimes unbracketed

Egyptian characteristics:
Little stroke contrast
Little or no stress
Thick, square serifs
Large x-height

Sans serif characteristics:
Some stroke contrast
Nearly vertical stress
Squarish curved strokes
Lower case *g* has open tail

Display typefaces do not possess a fixed number of characteristics.

Old Style

Transitional

Modern

Slab serif

Sans serif

Display

3

O

signs, accents, monetary symbols, and miscellaneous dingbats (assorted ornaments or fleurons designed for use in a font). Supplementing some desktop fonts are expert sets, which include characters such as small caps, a good selection of ligatures, fractions, and nonaligning figures. Minion Regular provides an excellent example of a font and its attendant expert set (fig. **4**).

The type family
A type family is a group of typefaces bound together by similar visual characteristics. Members of a family (typefaces) resemble one another, but also have their own unique visual traits. Typefaces within families consist of different weights and widths. Some type families consist of many members; others are composed of just a few. Extended families such as Stone include both serif and sans serif variations (fig. **5**).

Typographic measurement
The two primary units of measure in typography are the pica and the point. There are approximately six picas or 72 points to an inch; there are twelve points to a pica (fig. **6**). Points are used to specify the size of type, which includes the cap height of letters, plus a small interval of space above and below the letters. Typefaces of the same size may in fact appear different in size, depending on the size of the x-height. At the same size, letters with large x-heights appear larger than letters with smaller x-heights. Points are also used to measure the distance between lines; picas are used to measure the lengths of lines. The unit, a relative measure determined by dividing the em (which is the square of the type size), is used to reduce or increase the amount of space between letters, a process called tracking. Adjusting the awkward space between two letters to create consistency within words is called kerning.

The typographic grid
A typographic grid is used to aid the designer in organizing typographic and pictorial elements on a page and establishing unity among all of the parts of a design. Grids vary in complexity and configuration depending upon the nature of the information needing accommodation, and the physical properties of the typographic elements. Standard typographic grids possess flow lines, grid modules, text columns, column intervals, and margins (fig. **7**).

abcdefghijklmnopqrstuvwxyz
ABCDEFGHIJKLMNOPQRSTUVWXYZ&
ABCDEFGHIJKLMNOPQRSTUVWXYZ&
(.,;:,!?""''"~""\\´´´´^^ ~'""«»‹›- — —)
1234567890 1234567890 ($^{1234567890}/_{1234567890}$)
¼⅓½⅔¾⅝⅞%‰ [+√π=≠±≤≥÷∞°]
fffiflffiffl Œßæœ   \$£§¢
ÂÅÁÇÍÎÏØÓÒÔÚ áéíóúåäëïöüàèìòùâêîoû
¶‡†•⁎∧ ©™@

4

Stone Serif

Regular
Regular Italic
Semibold
Semibold Italic
Bold
Bold Italic

Stone Sans

Regular
Regular Italic
Semibold
Semibold Italic
Bold
Bold Italic

5

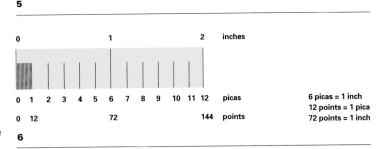

0			1			2		inches
0 1 2 3 4 5 6 7 8 9 10 11 12								picas
0 12		72			144			points

6 points = 1 inch
12 points = 1 pica
72 points = 1 inch

6

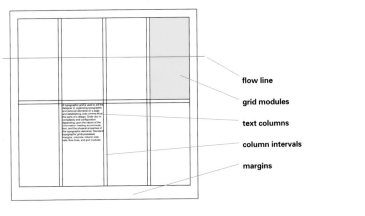

flow line
grid modules
text columns
column intervals
margins

7

SECURITE

ONLY FOR YOU: 1994

ONLY 4 YOU

19 94

FOR YOU

Greeting card 1994: *Only 4 You.* The words *only* and *you,* set in Template Gothic, are juxtaposed with a road sign in a desert setting reading *for you* to complete the card's message. Other typefaces include Frutiger and Variex.

5

Greeting card 1995: *The Five Senses* the numeral *9* joins with the *5* in ov complete the new year's date. Typo define the space; children taste, sm

Design:
David Shields

Client:
The Art Dept., a small art supply store in Memphis, Tennessee, offers a more personal alternative to the larger art supply centers in the city.

Concept:
This visually active and elastic identity system is based on the idea that the client could take over the design task once the first phase of the project was completed. Modular design components make it easy for the client (a non-designer) to adapt the system to different needs. The typographic exuberance conveys a sense of artistic play.

1

2

3

4

5

6

A repetition of vivid arcs emerges from

The distinctive logotype, based on a "serifed News Gothic" called Beach, is unified by a circle. The mark possesses an emblematic quality like that of a branding iron, which makes it strong and memorable. Used in some applications, a secondary version of the logotype has been transformed by filters into a floating, ghostly image.

Sometimes, a soft-edged crescent shape suggesting an artist's paint palette provides a background for the logotype. This form extends the art supply theme.

3
A detail from the business envelope reveals the painterly and expressive integration of the logotype and informational typography. The series of three vertical ruled lines aids in the organization of the information.

4
There is no question as to where on the envelope the stamp should be placed. This obvious overstatement contributes to the company's playful, creative atmosphere.

5
Texture is a key element in the personality of the identity. In this detail from the letterhead, which is typeset in Minion, typographic texture is achieved through generous tracking.

6
Newspaper advertisement.

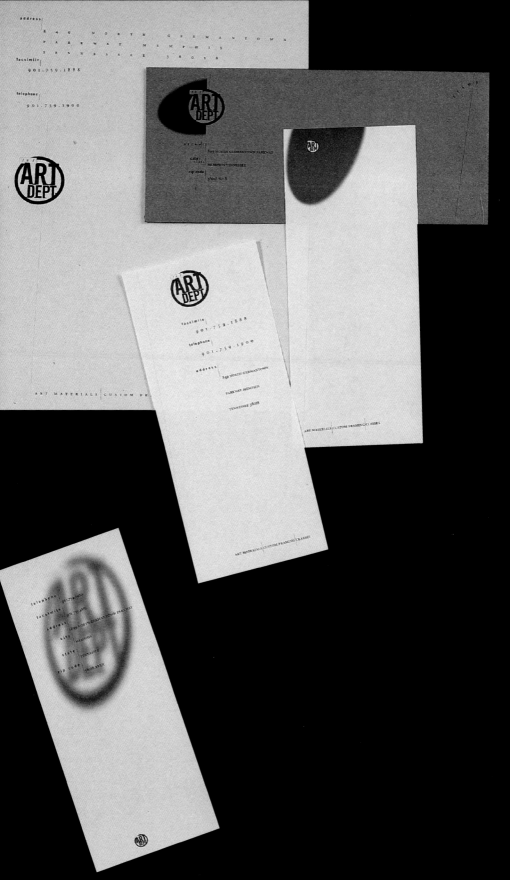

Design:
Brian Lane
30sixty design inc.

Art Direction:
Henry Vizcarra

Client:
Their own client, 30sixty design inc. is a ten-year-old design firm specializing in the entertainment industry. The firm's audience includes current clients, prospective clients, and design industry vendors.

Concept:
To achieve something different, the designers created a letterhead with message text conforming to the design rather than simply being a square block of type on the page. The colors of the identity program reflect the firm's environment, a studio located in verdant Hollywood Hills, California.

2

 30sixty design incorporated

2801 cahuenga blvd. west

los angeles, california 90068

1

3

4

1
Elemental graphic forms often provide bold and memorable signs. An emphatic *X* enclosed by an *O* suggests a symbol placed on a map to mark a significant point. The *X* appears to push beyond the restrictive boundaries of the *O,* referring perhaps to the vital energy and creativity of the design firm.

2
A detail of the business envelope reveals how the logotype, "OX" symbol, and curved line are joined to one another. Together these elements activate the space, providing it with movement and direction. A small but important detail is found in the precise alignment of the horizontal part of the curved line to the center point of the *X* to the mean line of the firm's name (shown by the blue dotted line). Integrated into the identity scheme is a subtle gradation that provides spatial depth.

3
This diagram illustrates how typed messages appearing on the letterhead conform to the ruled line bending from the top of the page to the bottom.

4
The identity's typeface is Bell Centennial, a highly legible face designed by Matthew Carter specifically for use in telephone books and at small sizes. This type is designed with spaces called "ink traps" notched out of letter strokes. These spaces increase legibility in poor printing and are noticeable only when the type is viewed at large sizes.

(X) 30sixty design

2801 cahuenga blvd. west

los angeles, california 90068

telephone [213] 850 5311

facsimile [213] 850 6618

modem [213] 850 5382

(X) 30sixty design incorporated

2801 cahuenga blvd. west

los angeles, california 90068

(X) 30sixty design incorporated

HENRY VIZCARRA

2801 cahuenga blvd. west

los angeles, california 90068

telephone [213] 850 5311

facsimile [213] 850 6618

modem [213] 850 5382

Design:
Lisa Levin
Jill Jacobson
Lisa Levin Design

Illustration:
Michael Schwab

Client:
Firedog Pictures is a children's video production company.

Concept:
The Dalmatian puppy seemed to be the perfect solution for a symbol representing this children's video production company. Always alert, loyal, and ready for action, this lovable pup represents the positive traits of the picture studio.

1 Some images possess qualities closely related to those of letterforms. The puppy image is effective visually because of the distinct black and white pattern, a quality found also in the form-counterform relationships of letters.

2 The logotype has the look of a "wine label" due to the traditional, centered alignment of the elements. The puppy illustration, which evokes the nostalgia of spot illustrations from the 1930s and 1940s, is framed in fire red. Curved placards contain the name of the studio, which is typeset in Bank Gothic.

3 Type placed on a curved base line draws attention to itself and acquires a kinetic quality in relationship to other less active elements. Compare the curved and uncurved examples. Curving type can be a very effective technique if it is not overdone. Note the fit of the squarish Bank Gothic letters and the curved rectangles.

4 Bauer Bodoni is used for the informational typography in the identity. It possesses elegant characteristics and refinements not found in other versions. Compare Bauer with another version of Bodoni.

5 Borders frame and formally enclose space. Use them in a manner that does not detract from key design elements. For the mailing label, a simple yellow band complements the logotype and address without distraction. The red border in the bottom example is too loud – like screaming at close range in someone's ear. It severely diminishes the impact of the logotype.

1

2

3

fg&j

fg&j

4

5

10 Hill Street · Mill Valley, California 94941
800-815-1234

10 Hill Street · Mill Valley, California 94941

Joe Matulich
President

159 East Blithedale Avenue
Mill Valley, California
94941
800-815-1234

Design:
Jean-Benoît Lévy
AND (Trafic Grafic)

Assistant:
Heinrich
Schaufelberger

Client:
Friends of the Bolshoi is a group of individuals and companies dedicated to the well-being and economic prosperity of the Bolshoi Ballet. This group aids the Bolshoi Foundation located in Geneva, Switzerland.

Concept:
Letters of two alphabets – an occidental *f* for friends, and a Cyrillic *b* for Bolshoi – combine as the primary logotype for Friends of the Bolshoi. The Bodoni *f* is printed in brown to denote warmth and friendship; the Б is printed in a cool green-blue for Russia. A secondary logotype physically links the words *Friends* and *Bolshoi* by means of vertical and horizontal ruled lines.

3

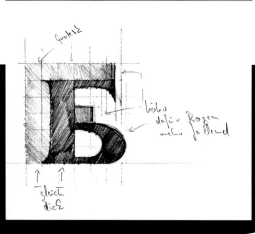

1

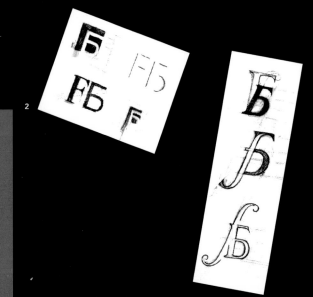

2

4

Jean-Benoît Lévy, living and practicing in Basel, Switzerland, developed this identity program based on a process of combining conceptual sketches made by hand with design refinements executed on computer. Initially, many sketches were made to explore a viable design direction.

Pencil sketches reveal early logotype development. One notation studies the visual relationships between a capital F with the Russian character Б.

Another study probes how these two characters might be combined into one form.

These sketches reveal further development of the logotype. A lower-case *f* replaces the capital F to explore its classical, dance like qualities.

On a laser proof of the nearly finalized logotype, the designer uses "white-out" for minute refinements.

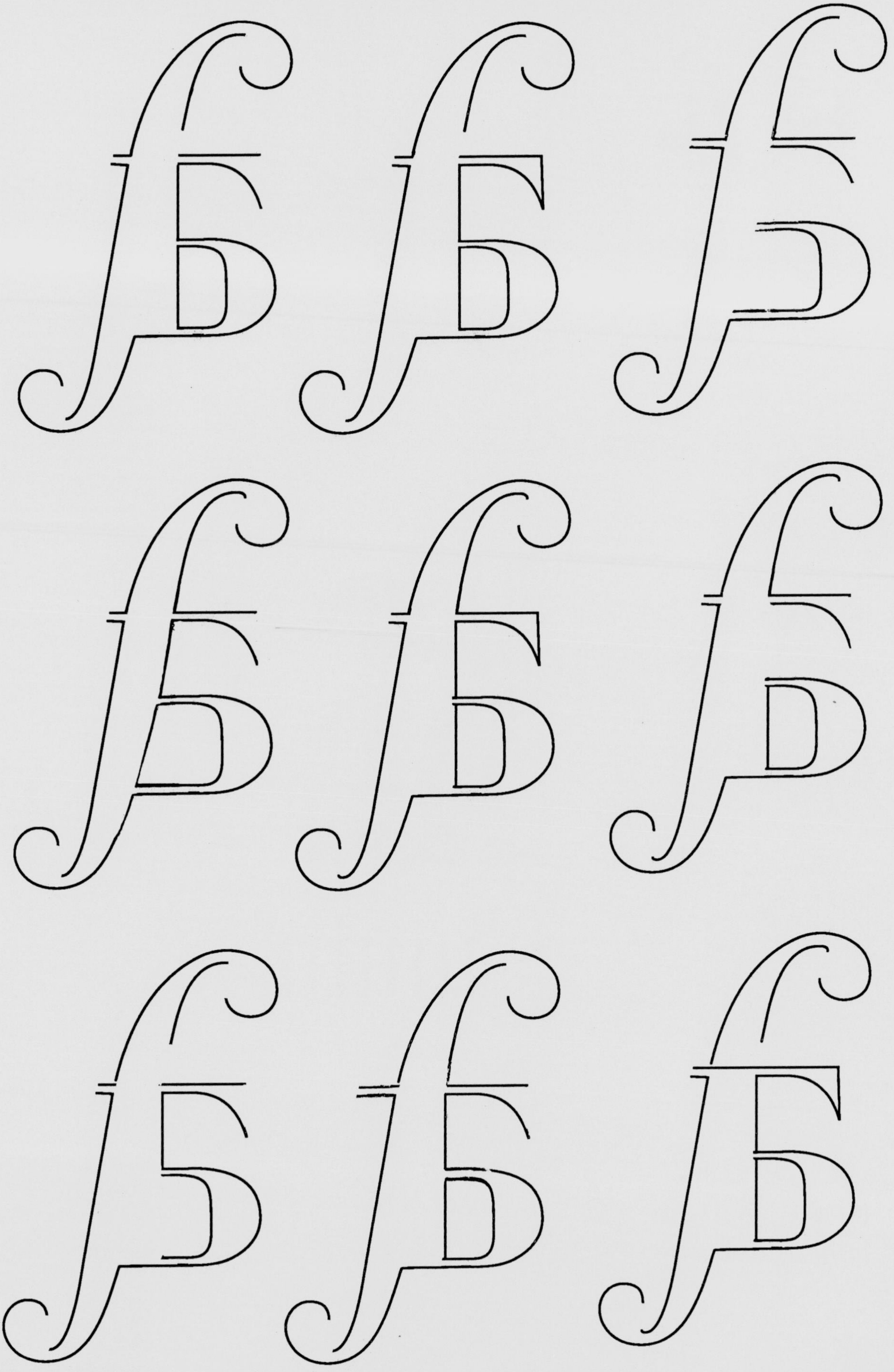

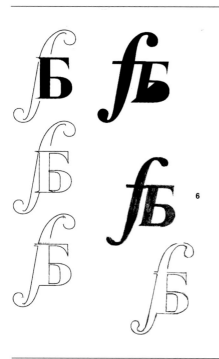

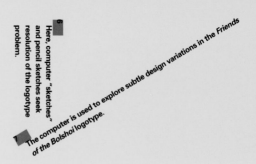

6

Here, computer "sketches" and pencil sketches seek resolution of the logotype problem.

7

The computer is used to explore subtle design variations in the Friends of the Bolshoi logotype.

6

8, 9

In the letterhead and envelope applications pictured on the facing page, you will notice that two complementary logotypes complete the system. The secondary logotype, which contains the name Bolshoi Ballet, was inspired by the architectural columns supporting the Bolshoi Ballet building. This is an apt metaphor for support offered by the "Friends of the Bolshoi." Letters composing the name of the organization are positioned between the "columns."

F R I E N D S
OF THE
B O L C H O I

F R I E N D S
OF THE
B O L C H O I

F R I E N D S
OF THE
B O L C H O I

F R I E N D S
OF
БОЛЬШОИ

7

8

F R I E N D S
OF
БОЛЬШОИ

FOUNDATION
" FRIENDS OF THE BOLSHOI "
1, PLACE ST. GERVAIS
CH - 1201 GENEVA

Design:
Jennifer Morla
Craig Bailey
Morla Design

Photo imaging:
Mark Eastman

Client:
San Francisco Production Group is a video production house specializing in design, animation, and special effects.

Concept:
The company is referred to as "SFPG", and it is upon this acronym that the design of the logotype is based. The energetic logotype references both the viewing vehicle, a television monitor, as well as a dialogue bubble in comic strips. On various applications, the logo teams with portrait images to playfully suggest the video medium.

Packaging for videocassettes and stationery items reveals flexibility in the use of the primary colors – red, yellow, and blue – and in the scale and position of the portraits. The large, full-bleed photos provide the system with visual drama.

In contrast to the flamboyant logotype and images, typography representing the company's vital information is set in unassuming blocks of Univers 63. This detail shows the information divided into logical units – set line-for-line – for optimum clarity.

Within applications, various "portraits" reference the range of video subjects represented in the studio. When these images are positioned in proximity to the logotype, they appear to be speaking the name of the studio.

Three typefaces – Bodoni, Boy Plain, and Franklin Gothic – were chosen for the logotype to represent the name of the company and to convey through their distinct visual personalities the spirit and variety of video animation. By themselves the letters provide little reference to the video studio; together they suggest the many voices in the world of video entertainment, and the letters form an explicit visual sign. The two offset bubbles, one boldly outlined in black and the other filled with solid yellow, enclose the letters to suggest movement and animation.

2

1

**San Francisco
Production Group**

**550 Bryant Street
San Francisco, CA 94107
phone: (415) 495.5595
fax: (415) 543.8370**

3

38
39

Margo Chase
Margo Chase Design

Bradley Group Inc. specializes in sales and support of Macintosh-based systems for broadcast design, nonlinear video editing, video and TV post-production, print design, and advertising.

The flying eye/wing image used in the logotype is a symbol for "speedy visuals," the fast delivery of service by the Bradley Group. A custom font named Bradley, designed by Margo Chase, is set off with sophisticated colors for an uncommon, personalized image.

1

2

Two elements establish the logotype: a specially drawn capital letter B, and the space eye/wing symbol. A blade-like shape of black sweeping across the space contains the logotype and provides an air of mystery. Above, the logotype is viewed in color and in outline form as created on the computer. The sombre but rich colors were chosen to illustrate the sophisticated image of the company.

2

Bradley, the typeface, provides the identity with sophistication. It is a distinctive face resembling some of the Art Nouveau typefaces used by the designer Will Bradley at the turn of the century. When set into text, Bradley is both serious and sensual. In the various applications, it is generously letter spaced.

3

An unusual feature of the identity system is the irregular, curvilinear shapes of the stationery. Die-cut edges conforming to the black shapes give each item a distinctly curved edge. This device contributes to the mannerist tone of the identity. The flowing curves characterizing the identity would be less effective were it not for the rectilinear placement of the text type. Lines of type meeting at right angles provide a contrast that accentuates the curved elements.

B r a d l e y

B R A D L E Y group

6666 hollywood boulevard suite 229 hollywood california 90028 213-465-7593 fax 213-465-7679

3

B

blvd suite 229 hollywood ca 90028

6646 hollywood

213-465-7593
fax 213-465-7679

B R A D L E Y group

james bradley

6646 hollywood blvd #229
hollywood ca 90028

Design:
Cheryl Brzezinski-
Beckett
Minor Design Group

Client:
Owned by women, the Powell Group is a leading dealer of premier office furniture, systems, and accessories. The company represents Knoll furniture and offers fine modernist classics such as the Barcelona and Eames chairs.

Concept:
The Powell Group's identity is a statement of the client's interest in Modernist form and space. Printed materials represent the clean and sparse aesthetic found in the firm's furniture and space planning.

1

The|Powell|Group

2

The|Powell|Group

The|Powell|Group

5599 San Felipe
Suite 555
Houston, Tx 77056

■ 5599 San Felipe
Suite 555
Houston, Tx 77056
Fax: 713 . 629 . 4600
713 . 629 . 5599

The|Powell|Group

5599 San Felipe
Suite 555
Houston, Tx 77056
Fax 713 . 629 . 4600
713 . 629 . 5599

Century Expanded, designed at the turn of the century, is open and clean yet warm and friendly. Hinting slightly of tradition, it represents the firm's established reputation. It is one of those old, trustworthy typefaces that is worth dusting off on occasion.

1
The logotype, which features Century Expanded as the primary typeface, references through a simple arrangement of type and vertical ruled lines the concept of space planning. As the ruled lines suggest interior divisions of space or partitions, they also divide and separate the three words composing the firm's name.

2
Details showing three variations in the use of the logotype. The "modular" identity system allows for various adaptations of the logotype, supporting ruled lines, and information blocks.

The name "Powell" is accentuated with red for a more distinctive and memorable typographic image. The black-red-black combination is a simple but effective example of ABA form, a term referring to the important principle of

repetition and contrast. Implementing this principle brings both harmony and variety to type.

3
A red square is a theme used consistently throughout identity materials. It effectively punctuates and emphasizes information such as the firm's address on the letterhead. It is also used as an "arrow" to mark the placement of a written letter on the letterhead and mailing address on the envelope. The back of the business card is printed in solid red to further reference the square. In a brochure for the firm, the red square frames images of chairs and other furniture.

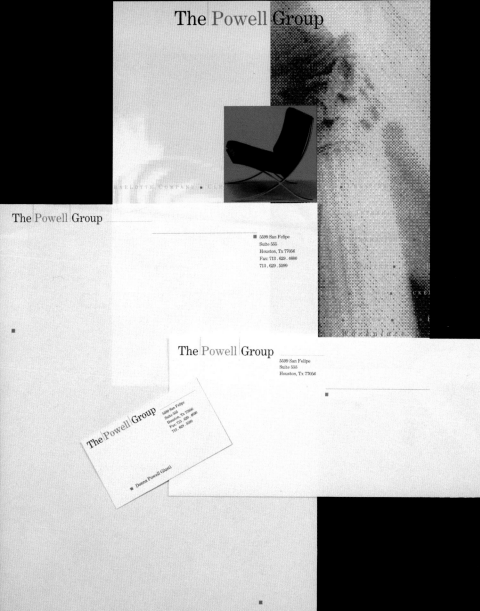

Design:
Ingeborg Bloem
Visser Bay Anders
Toscani

Creative direction:
Teun Anders

Photography:
Reinoud Klazes

Client:
Breda Fotografica is an annual photography exhibition in Breda, Holland that attracts the works of innovative photographers from around the world.

Concept:
The large scale and diversity of this exhibition require a unifying identity. For the 1993 exhibition, a dramatic burning fish serves as the central image, a symbol of antithesis and surprise in contemporary photographic art. A logotype appears on all of the exhibition materials. This mark alludes to the mechanical properties of a camera and the visual process of making photographs.

1

3

4

5

Two sans serif typefaces form the Breda Fotografica logotype: Din Mittelschrift and News Gothic. Both are condensed, clean, and monostroke faces with simple characteristics. The precise distinct word *FOTO*, with its establishes a pattern of letters, centerpiece for the logotype. (Note the rhythmic alternating pattern of the letters *F* vertical/horizontal letter and *T*, and the circular letter *O*.) As the letters in *FOTO* increase gradually in size, they are split by a "wedge of light," a reference to the photographic process. The letters *GRAFICA* emanate from the light to produce a visually seductive mark. The logotype is accentuated further with a red dot enclosing *BREDA* and the letter *F*.

1
Each annual exhibition centers on themes that broaden the scope of the identity. The "burning fish" is the primary image for the 1993 exhibition, and it serves as a visual link between the various subthemes. The general poster reveals an integration of the logotype, fish image, and informational typography. Other typefaces used in this poster and various exhibition materials are Officina Sans, Rotis Sans, and OCR-A.

3–5
Exhibition catalog (top), festival newsletter (middle), and flyer (bottom).

2
General poster (facing page)

06 | 07
™
19 | 09

FOTO
GRAFICA
BREDA

internationale
stromingen in fotobeeld

Fotografie en de computer

Japanse fotografie in

heden en verleden

Hedendaags Nederlands fotowerk

Actueel internationaal fotobeeld

Te zien op 15 lokaties in Breda

2

Theme posters incorporated into the identity include: a fish appearing as steel and microchips for *Photography and the Computer;* a fish appearing as a splash of water for *Present International Photoworks;* and finally, a fish imprinted in beach sand for *Contemporary Dutch Photography,* since Holland begins where the sea ends; and finally, a tattooed fish for *Japanese Photography: Past and Present.* Although typographic treatments vary from one poster to another, a consistent presentation of the logotype and fish images links them together as a system.

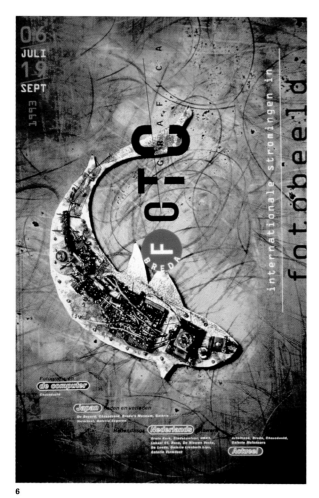

6

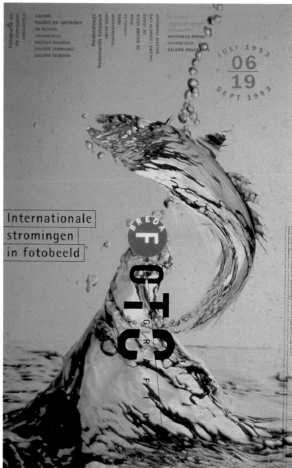

7

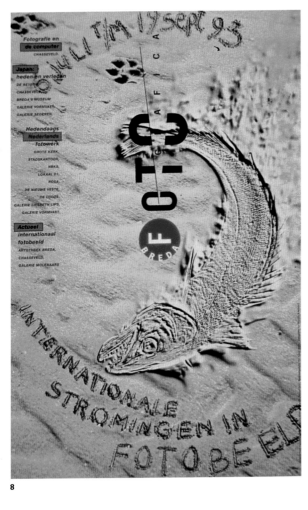

8

9

Design:
Carlos Segura
Segura Inc.

Photography:
Pedro Lobo

Client:
Confetti Magazine, the client for this visual identity program, holds an annual computer-generated art show called *Digital Dynamite* that features design, illustration, and photography. Segura Inc. designs the show's "call for entries."

Concept:
The identity was developed to capture the digital theme of the show. "Exploding" with visual energy, the logotype is used in concert with highly charged imagery. The use of the typefaces Flammable Solid by Carlos Segura, and Tetsuo Organic by Eric Lin, supports the show's outrageous slant.

1

4

3

2

A logotype, designed to tie together advertisements and other materials for the computer design show, visually "explodes" in a pyrotechnic array of letterforms, lines, and shapes. The word *digital* is divided into three units, a device that provides the logotype with rhythmic energy and enables it to be read doubly as "dig it all". The concoction of shapes composing the logotype appears to expand outward from the center, and "flames" viewed on the logotype's horizon heighten the visual effect. The central typeface used in the logotype is Flammable by Carlos Segura; announcement text in calls for entries features Tetsuo Organic by Eric Lin.

2
A call for entries occupying a spread in *Confetti Magazine* integrates the logotype into a vibrant field of form, texture, and color. The effect projects visual energy and excitement.

3
Tetsuo Organic possesses distorted qualities that seem to fit the concept of this campaign. It is a member of a growing family of eccentric and expressive faces that are meant to be viewed as much as read.

4
The reader is confronted with the image of a slingshot aimed dead at the face. The metaphorical ammunition is a globe of the world. This image conceptually augments the dynamite theme.

5
A textured video image of an open mouth calls for action and participation. Enlarged fragments of the detonated logotype blast forward into space.

THE IDEA.
The best computer-generated art samples from today's creative minds.
DESIGN. ILLUSTRATION. PHOTOGRAPHY.
Show us how you pushed the limits, what software and hardware you used, and which configuration.
Show us the outrageous, the original and the inventive.
Just don't show us anything less than digital dynamite.

dig it al
DYNAMITE

call for entry information
800.4 1.8166
deadline - October 15th, 1993!

Design:
Jerry Hutchinson
Hutchinson
Associates, Inc.

Client:
Graphics Suisse Inc. is a small paper distributor in Chicago, exclusively representing the Sihl paper mills of Zurich, Switzerland.

Concept:
The swatchbook presents samples of a line of translucent papers. The identity, which binds all of the papers into a unified presentation, refers to the Swiss origins of the paper, and demonstrates the printability of solid inks and halftones.

Graphics Suisse Inc.

gsi

Sihl

1

Formata

Formata

2

3

1
A cohesive identity is established in the pages of the swatchbook through the use of a design framework based on the Swiss cross (shown in the diagram) – an emblem that also establishes the primary visual theme of the book.

2
The consistent use of the typefaces Formata and Rotis Serif contributes to the unity of the book. Formata Outline, appearing hollow and transparent, relates visually to the properties of the paper presented in the swatchbook. The choice of typeface can and most often does have a synergistic relationship with the content of a message. Compare the solid and outline versions of Formata.

cross with a circle, and contained within the cross is a negative image of trees that provides a dramatic texture.

To avoid confusion, the system dictates that the names of the various papers be placed vertically in proximity to the vertical stroke of the cross. Likewise, the weight and color designations of the paper are always positioned horizontally in proximity to the horizontal stroke of the cross.

3
GSI swatchbook cover.

4–6
Representative pages from the GSI swatchbook showing the identity system.

The variations on the cross theme enliven the system as they occur from page to page. A variety of photographs printed inside the cross provides contrast and texture, while ruled lines and shapes playfully mingle.
On one page, overlapping white rectangles distort the cross, which contains a whirling photograph of gears. Another page combines the

SihlClear print

62lb.

4

SihlClear Print.62lb.

Graphics Suisse Inc.
1.800.944.7445

blue

SihlClear marbled

88lb.

SihlClear Marbled Blue.62lb.

Graphics Suisse Inc.
1.800.944.7445

5

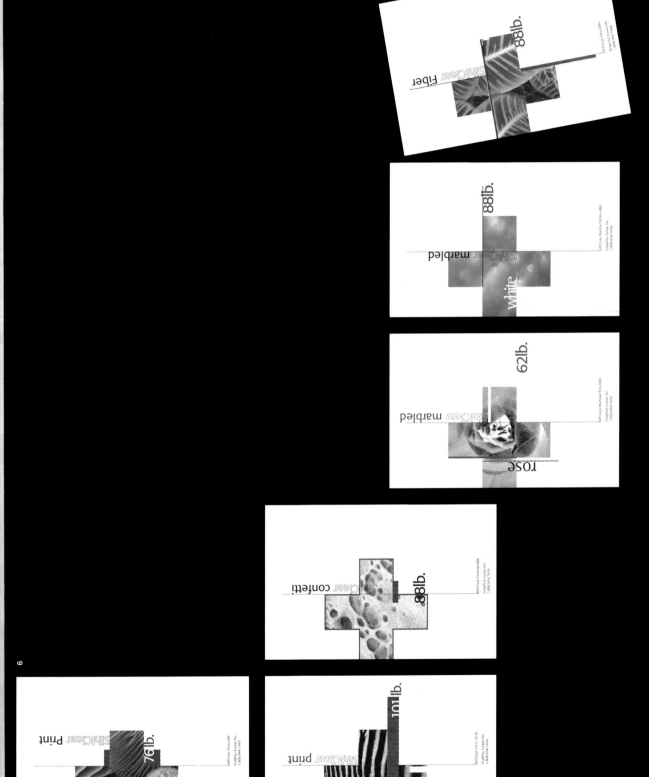

Design:
Alexander Isley
Alexander Isley Design

Client:
The American Museum of the Moving Image, a public museum located in New York City, focuses on time-based media such as film, television, video, and interactive media. The Museum offers film and video screenings, presentations, and tours.

Concept:
Applied to everything from program guides to baseball caps and cups, the logotype is an image suggesting the frames in film. Each letter of the acronym AMMI is assigned to a quadrant of a square defined by a horizontal and vertical line. What makes the logotype memorable is a visual pun that substitutes the letter *I* with an image of a human eye.

Franklin Gothic

3

1

2   4

Several design features contribute to the effectiveness of the logotype. Horizontal and vertical lines form a + sign (always a connotation of the positive). This form also provides a structure for the placement of the letters *AMM* and the eye image. The boldness of the Franklin Gothic Roman letters imbues the mark with visual strength; and the repetition of the two *M*s establishes a unifying and memorable pattern.

Shown here are two versions of the logotype – the basic version and a more elaborate variation encircled by the name of the organization.

5

the more elaborate version is based on a circle enclosing a square.

Often, the most effective logotypes are those based on the simplest shapes. The basic AMMI logotype is constructed from a square;

The eye is not only a clever visual pun for the letter *i*, it is an image substituting for the word *image*. Obviously, it functions also as a sign for seeing.

The circular typography "moves" cinematically around the other elements, reinforcing the idea of moving images. Separating the type into two distinct typefaces and weights makes it easier to read. Several software applications enable type to be wrapped around circular paths. When it comes to computer special effects, reason and common sense find no substitute.

The logotype applied to a baseball cap and coffee mug.

The AMMI's *Quarterly Guide to Exhibitions & Programs.*

Design:
Peter Martin

Digital animation:
Peter Martin

Client:
A prototype for an educational program, Tandem 3 aims to provide memorable learning experiences for college students who combine physical outdoor activity such as wilderness treks with participatory community projects and computer-assisted instruction.

Concept:
The identity for this organization serves as a metaphor for change and development as it occurs in students participating in the program. Viewed on a computer screen as animated titling, it identifies various stages of instruction and visually suggests the progress of the students.

1 Early in the process, the computer is used to sketch typographic ideas. The name *Tandem 3* is warped and skewed, fragmented and deconstructed. These studies test the limits of legibility and explore relationships between form and meaning.

2 The lines and dots in the top example represent a study of the structure of the name *Tandem 3* (bottom). This experimentation gives the designer a better sense of the visual rhythms contained within the word picture (a term referring to the visual rather than verbal attributes of a word). These attributes are applied to further investigation. Covering all bases, *Tandem 3* is set into several different typefaces for observation.

3 Computer sketches lead to variations of the basic logotype (pictured in the lower right-hand corner of the facing page). These variations within the system are applied to specific courses within the program.

4 A schematic map calculatingly traces the movements of logotype elements as they appear on the computer screen. The animated sequence shown on the facing page reflects these movements.

5 This is the animated logotype as it appears on the computer screen. Moving lines, planes, and type establish a dynamic visual field, a metaphor for individual growth and change as it occurs in students enrolled in the educational program.

tandem 3
tandem 3
tandem 3
tandem 3
tandem 3
tandem 3

1

tandem 3

2

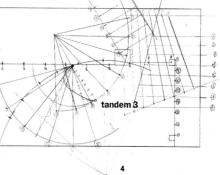

tandem 3

4

3

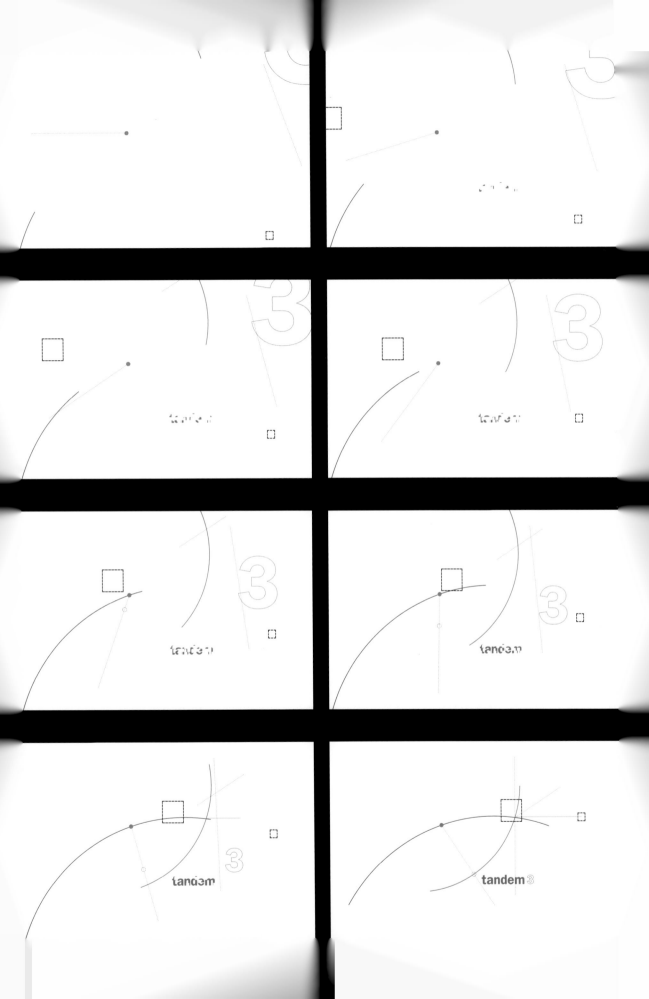

April Greiman
Greimanski Labs

RoTo Architects, Inc., an architectural firm
practicing internationally, engages in diverse
projects that range in scope and budget.

The logotype, based on the name RoTo, varies
in appearance from application to application.
The name itself possesses memorable
qualities, such as the sound of the word when
spoken, and the distinct repetition of the two
os. Wide letter spacing and elements spread
horizontally through the space suggest built
forms in the landscape.

1

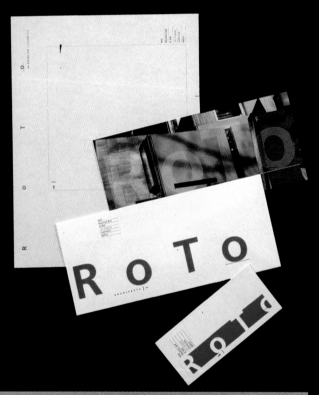

Sometimes an existing identity program must be changed or replaced with some-thing new and
fresh. For whatever reason an identity changes, the ultimate goal is to provide an image that best
represents an organization...image is everything. Compare RoTo Architects' earlier identity,
presented on this page, with the new one shown on the facing page. In both versions, the identity
focuses on a typographic/architectonic setting rather than on the integration of a specific mark.

The retired program is a
typographic environment
possessing "built" qualities.
The name RoTo functions
always as the dominant
element in applications, and it
appears in great variety.
There is also consistency,
such as the treatment of the
address block where parts are
separated by thin ruled lines.
Red and black are the
recurrent colors. In most
uses, RoTo appears in red (or
reversed from red to appear
as white), and it stretches in
an even cadence across the space. The R and T are
capitalized; the o and o are set in lower case. Pronounced
size changes in the name of the firm occur from application
to application.

2
The new retains something of the old. The visual theme remains p
architectural in tone, although the recent version suggests an
expansive, poetic architectural landscape; the typeface (Frutiger) is
retained; and the second o in RoTo is underscored with a ruled line
before. Changes do occur in typographic detail and color, and a sma
horizontal photograph integrates with typography.

fashion – purple
pka.

[ ] elia najem
photography
0771 557 0 292
www.elianajem.com

Lifestyle
people
Abstract
B & W .

pdf.
CMYK 28 pi
.pdf

portrait
still life
abstract
wedding

photographer
0171 5570 392

www.elianajem.co.uk

600
Moulton Ave
305
Los Angeles
California
90031

fax 213 226 1105 213 226 1112

O I

A R C H I T E C T S

michael Rotondi Principal
R D T O   ARCHITECTS INC
ROTOARK@AOL.COM

fax 213 226 1105

Design:
Jean-Benoît Lévy
AND (Trafic Grafic)

Client:
Suter Unternehmens und
Wirtschaftsberatung, a consultancy,
analyzes the economic strengths and
weaknesses of private individuals and
companies and provides solutions for
financial growth and improvement.

Concept:
The logotype, consisting of a stripe and the
letter *S*, represents the financial consultation
process. The stripe, representing a company in
need of a financial consultant, intersects the *S*
(for Suter, the President of the consulting firm).
Upon meeting the *S*, the stripe continues on,
having symbolically moved ahead financially.

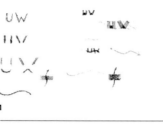

1

Designer Jean-Benoît Lévy
begins the design process
with rudimentary pencil
sketches. Soon, the computer
aids in a more specific search
for answers. Ideas surface,
join other ideas, and
disappear for a time, only to
reappear in another form.

Laser proofs reveal preliminary logotype investigations along a single conceptual
theme: the idea of two intersecting parts referring to a meeting of consultant
and client. A viable solution begins to take shape. The computer enables
immediate viewing of subtle letterform relationships that can be evaluated and
tweaked for clarity.

2

3

Further development yields fruitful results as the final logotype – the intersecting *S* (for Suter) – begins to blossom. Confidently, it is tested for the first time in an application, as shown in the bottom part of the example.

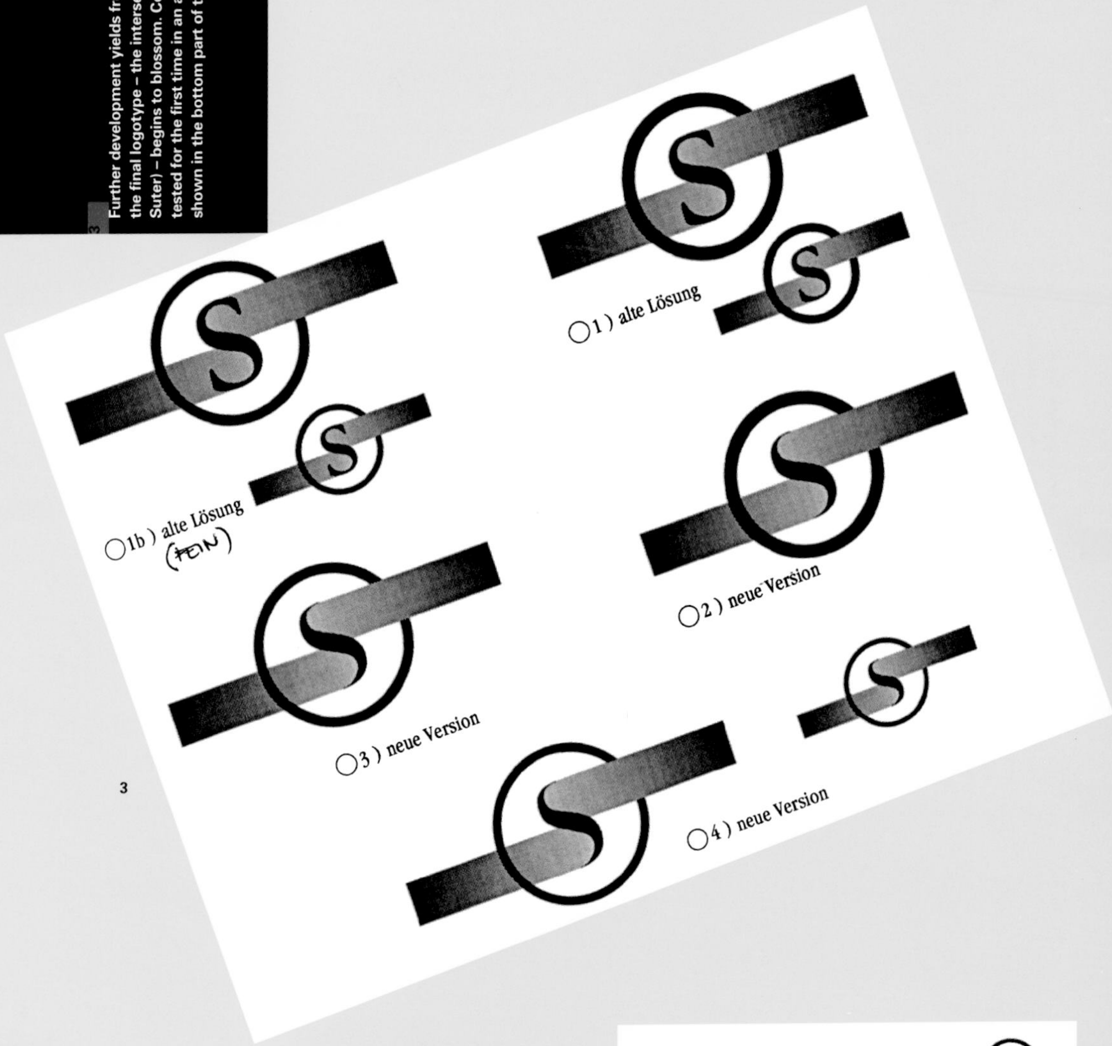

3

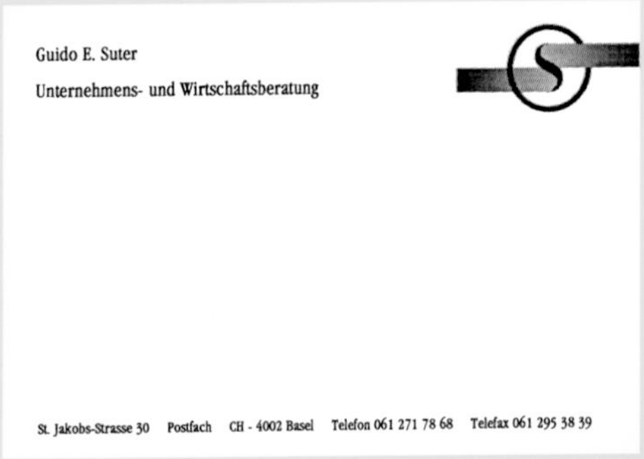

○ 1) alte Lösung

○ 1b) alte Lösung
(ꟼoꟼ)

○ 2) neue Version

○ 3) neue Version

○ 4) neue Version

Guido E. Suter
Unternehmens- und Wirtschaftsberatung

St. Jakobs-Strasse 30   Postfach   CH - 4002 Basel   Telefon 061 271 78 68   Telefax 061 295 38 39

4

The final logotype and its integration into representative business materials.

The final version of the logotype is taken through a series of color studies. To explore gradient color fills in the bars projecting from the S, old-fashioned paint is thoughtfully applied to black and white laser proofs. A low-resolution color printer proves an excellent tool for testing numerous color combinations.

ALLES
WIRD MIT VERLÄUFEN
SEIN.

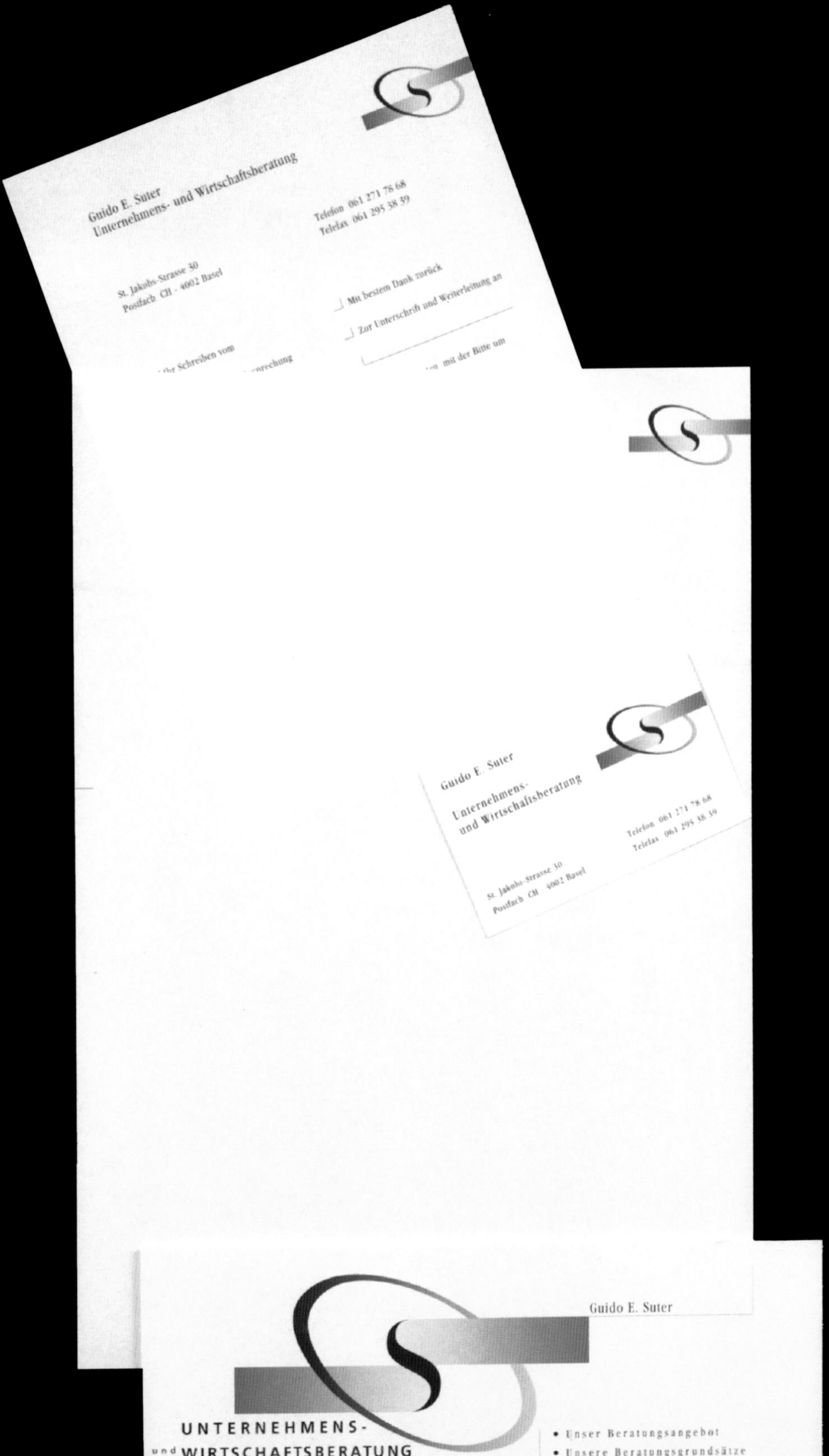

Guido E. Suter
Unternehmens- und Wirtschaftsberatung

Telefon 061 271 78 68
Telefax 061 295 38 59

St. Jakobs-Strasse 50
Postfach CH - 4002 Basel

Mit bestem Dank zurück

Zur Unterschrift und Weiterleitung an

hr Schreiben vom   erechnung   m mit der Bitte um

Guido E. Suter

Unternehmens-
und Wirtschaltsberatung

Telefon 061 271 78 68
Telefax 061 295 38 59

St. Jakobs-Strasse 50
Postfach CH 4002 Basel

Guido E. Suter

UNTERNEHMENS-
und WIRTSCHAFTSBERATUNG

• Unser Beratungsangebot
• Unsere Beratungsgrundsätze
• Unsere Methodik

Design:
Communication
Design, Inc.

Client:
B&B Printing is a family-owned company whose visual facelift helped to reposition them in the competitive world of high-end corporate printing. Their original "homespun" logo was shed for a more contemporary and professional image.

Concept:
In designing the logotype, the designers were directed by the client to visually preserve the name *B&B*, which holds a lot of equity for this long-established firm. In addition to the task of visually preserving the name, the rounded strokes of the two Extra Bold Futura *B*s suggest the ink rollers on a printing press.

The bold, geometric appearance of Futura contrasts effectively with the curvilinear Century Schoolbook to provide a logotype of visual distinction. Dozens of fonts were tested to determine just the right combination.

Red was selected for the logotype to differentiate the client from competitors. A casual survey of local competition revealed that no area printers use red as their corporate color.

1 An ampersand, set in Century Schoolbook, links the two Futura Extra Bold *B*s to form a memorable ligature (a term used to describe two or more characters touching one another).

2 The use of Futura Extra Bold enabled the ampersand to be reversed out of the twin *B*s to appear as white. The use of any other weight of Futura would eliminate this possibility. Weight, which is the lightness or heaviness of a typeface, is determined by the ratio of the stroke thickness to character height. Displayed in descending order are the five basic weights of Futura: Extra Bold, Bold, Heavy, Regular, Light.

3 In most of the identity applications, the full name of the firm appears together with the logotype. Times Roman, all capitals, was chosen for this task, for it provides a traditional counterpoint to the more progressive, contemporary logotype.

4 One of the most effective uses of the computer is to establish precise visual relationships between letters. Consider the careful scaling of the ampersand and its precise alignment to the two upper-case *B*s. Arrows point to critical junctions between forms. Notice also how the curve of the ampersand's bottom counter matches perfectly the curve of the *B*.

1

B B B B B 2

3 B&B PRINTING

4

B&B PRINTING
521 Research Road
Richmond, Virginia 23236
NOTES
B&B
B&B PRINTING
521 Research Road
Richmond, Virginia 23236
804-794-8273
804-379-4961

Design:
Bart Crosby
Crosby Associates Inc.

Client:
Typographic Resource, a Chicago-based service bureau, provides its customers with typesetting, pre-press production, and proofing.

Concept:
The Tr. logotype carries a double meaning: it stands for Typographic Resource and it is a proofreader's mark for transposition. Futura and Akzidenz Grotesk, both clean and classical type families, work well for this grid-oriented identity program.

2

3

Typographic Resource

1

Tr.

A *T*, an *r*, and a dot. Three letterforms, unremarkable and unpretentious by themselves, combine into an intensely direct, visually fertile mark. While utterly simple in appearance, the mark is in reality based on carefully articulated visual relationships: 1) The use of Futura Extra Bold Condensed letters; 2) the proximity of the letters to each other; 3) the verticality of the stems of the *T* and *r*; 4) the transition in shape from the horizontal stroke of the *T* to the circular tail of the *r*, and then to the round dot; 5) the matching diameter of the dot to the stroke widths of the letters. Each of these characteristics contributes to a remarkable typographic sign.

2

This diagram reveals some of the intricate visual relationships of the *Tr.* logotype. Observe the unifying square (indicated in yellow) formed by the strokes of the *T* and *r* and the space between them.

3

A consistent feature of the identity system is the placement of the firm's name adjacent the *Tr.* logotype. Both elements are typeset in the same face, size, and weight. The two elements in juxtaposition establish a kind of question/answer relationship. *Tr.* poses the question "What is Tr. ?"; *Typographic Resource* answers the question.

4–6

These applications reveal the consistent organizational strategy of the system. Long, horizontal ruled lines divide pages into spatial bands occupied by specific information. This device is supported by a traditional typographic grid. Dynamic scale contrasts, the use of solid red backgrounds, and abundant white space distinguish the identity system.

4

5

**A newsletter for type enthusiasts
from Typographic Resource**

2

3

4

Contents
Why Choose Berthold?
Berthold Bodoni – IBM's new
corporate typeface
New typefaces
Comparison of typefaces by period
List of text typefaces available from
Typographic Resource
Reduction horizontal and vertical scale
Range of point sizes

Typographic Resource

Typographic Resource

Tr.

Tr.

Tr.

Lisa M. Helmstetter

Kinetics is an annual festival of film and video titling. At the heart of this competitive event is the imaginative use of moving type and image.

Letters and lines converge actively to suggest movement and the physical properties of film as it threads through a projector. Use of the primary colors red, yellow, and blue intensifies the kinetic effect.

Futura

Representative sketches indicate the range of early logotype investigation. The word *kinetics* is outlined and then fragmented in an attempt to reveal movement and activity among the lines composing the letters; the letter *k* is reduced to lines of varying weights, and shifted at an angle.

5

The tickets for the event are long and narrow in shape, suggesting strips of film. A gradient fill in the background heightens the kinetic and dimensional appearance.

4

The identity system is quite flexible in that the logotype is capable of subtle visual transformation as it is applied to different materials. Ruled lines are added and subtracted as needed. For videotape packaging, the lines are increased in size for contrast.

2

The gateway to the final logotype was a thorough investigation of the word/line theme. Several typefaces were tested for their visual effectiveness.

For the logotype, the word *kinetics* emerges from a parade of yellow, green, red, and blue ruled lines. The color and cadence of the lines suggest vibration, movement and rhythm.

kinetics

1

3 kinetics

kinetics

kinetics

kinetics

kinetics

kinetics

Kinetics

Kinetics

2

kinetics

kinetics

annual
film
festival

May 22, 1996
Byrd Theatre
Richmond, VA

5

4

Design:
Takaaki Matsumoto
Matsumoto
Incorporated

Client:
A non profit organization, the International Design Network Foundation brings together various branches of the international design community.

Concept:
The connected Futura letters composing the logotype represent the mission of the organization – the unification of the various design disciplines. The use of vivid red in the organization's stationery provides the identity system with visual vitality.

IDNF ²

1

3

4

Several features provide this logotype with visual appeal. Among them are the joining of the outlined letters to create a single open, pleasing silhouette; the rhythmic progression of the letters from large to small; and the single, half-circle creating an island within the space.

2 Futura Extra Bold letters offer an appropriate weight and shape necessary for the logotype to work visually. Thinner letters or letters of another typeface would yield an entirely different look. An awareness of the visual attributes inherent in different typefaces aids the designer in identifying the best faces for a given task. Shown are the letters before computer manipulation.

3 Here you see the position of the letters in relationship to each other before the overlapping strokes were removed. Just the right sizing and just the right spacing are critical concerns.

4 The logotype filled in black clearly shows the overall shape of the overlapping letters. The actual logotype, expressed as an outlined form, relates best to the "unification" concept, for the lines join one another in unity.

5 The stationery system shows how the logotype is integrated into the greater identity program. Informational text is typeset in Courier, a nuts and bolts typeface resembling typewriter type. The layout, reflecting the openness of the logotype, is light and airy.

International
Design
Network
Foundation

International
Design
Network
Foundation

International
Design
Network
Foundation

International
Design
Network
Foundati

Yoshiko Ebihara
Founding Director

International
Design   91 Grand Street
Network   New York, NY 10013
Foundation   212.334.4363
                212.219.1684 Fax

International
Design
Network
Foundation

6

5

Joyce Munn
Secretary and
Educational Program Director

...national

91 Grand St...
New Y...

...Street
...Y 10013

Takaaki Matsumoto
Matsumoto
Incorporated

The Worldesign Foundation is a nonprofit organization that advocates growth and development of the international design community.

The logotype is a visual metaphor for the globe, signifying the international scope of the Foundation. The different weights of letters in the logotype create an illusion of perspective and suggest the spherical shape of the earth.

1

WOR**LDE**SIGN

3

WOR**LDE**SIGN

3
The effect of this letterform arrangement can be compared with the calculated transition from light to dark to light in a tonal gradation.

2
In applications, the logotype is printed in green, a color symbolizing growth, fresh-ness, youth, and vigor. Informational typography appears in blue. The identity colors evoke calmness and harmony, desirable traits for a worldwide design organi-zation. Stationery reveals a refined and understated identity system. Bodoni adds a distinctive texture by functioning as the typeface for informational text. Plentiful white space illumi-nates the type elements and adds a touch of sophistication (facing page).

1
This logotype is a testament to the elasticity of the Futura family and the skill of the designer. Beginning with the *W* in *WORLD,* which is set in Futura Light, type ascends in weight to the *D,* and then descends in reverse order to the *N* in *DESIGN.* The progression in weight is smooth and deliberate, as in the curvature of a sphere. Working with type in a skillful manner such as this requires a knowledge of type families and a sensitivity to their visual nuances. Not all type families consist of as many weights as Futura.

Another distinguishing feature of the logotype is the letter *D,* which is shared by the words *WORLD* and *DESIGN.* This letter, set in the heaviest weight of Futura, establishes the visual center of the mark.

WORLDESIGN

Worldesign Foundation Inc.
1142-E Walker Road
Great Falls, Virginia 22066 USA

WOR**LDE**SIGN

Peter Edward Lowe, FIDSA
Vice President & Trustee

WOR**LDE**SIGN Worldesign Foundation Inc.
1142-E Walker Road
Great Falls, Virginia 22066 USA
Telephone 703.759.0100
Facsimile 703.759.7679

WOR**LDE**SIGN

WOR**LDE**SIGN

Worldesign Foundation Inc.
1142-E Walker Road
Great Falls, Virginia 22066 USA
Telephone 703.759.0100
Facsimile 703.759.7679

WOR**LDE**SIGN

Worldesign Foundation Inc.
1142-E Walker Road
Great Falls, Virginia 22066 USA

Board of T
Donald
Andrew
Vice P
David D. T
Secretary/T
Robert T. S
Executive

Peter W. B
James F.
Nunzo G
David J
Ross Lov
Peter Edwar
Kenneth M
Tsutomu "Tom" M
Randolph McAu
Nancy R. N
Louis N
Ralph F. Osterhout
Glenn Potter, Ph.D.
Deane W. Richardson
Beatrice Rivas-Sanchez
James M. Ryan
Craig M. Vogel
Peter H. Wooding

WOR**LDE**SIGN

2

Design:
John Muller
Muller + Company

Client:
The Main Street Garage Vintage Race Team restores and races old automobiles in the nostalgic traditions of the past.

Concept:
The emblematic logotype for the racing team is a stylized *M* based on the typeface Futura Extra Bold. Complete with tire treads and wings, this Retro mark resembles the Art Deco motifs of an earlier era.

1

M M

2

3

The streamlined logotype, an emblem of immense pride and competition, consists of three "component parts" (car mechanic vernacular): 1) a shield shape for protection against one's competitors; 2) the name of the racing team framed tightly between horizontal ruled lines (Retro Vienna Secession trait); and 3) a winged *M* for *Main Street Garage.* Perhaps this sign, reminiscent of Art Deco forms from the 1920s and 1930s, also connotes masculinity, virility, power, and freedom – desirable traits of a vintage race car driver.

While the name of the racing team is typeset in Futura, the winged *M* more closely approximates a Gill Sans Extra Bold *M* with its two vertical stems. Though Gill Sans was not specifically singled out as the design model for the winged *M*, it is nonetheless important to realize that the more knowledge you have of specific letter traits, the more you are able to adapt letters to solutions of design problems. Compare a Futura Extra Bold *M* (top) with a Gill Sans Extra Bold *M* (bottom).

5

Depending on the application, the winged *M* can appear with or without the shield shape. Here you see it applied to clothing, helmets, and cars.

Design:
Nancy Nowacek

Client:
The Learning Web is a non-profit youth outreach program sponsored by Cornell University in Ithaca, New York. The focus of the organization is experiential education, which aids youth in becoming participating members of their communities and in identifying potential career possibilities.

Concept:
The identity program centers on a symbol that abstractly represents the Learning Web's philosophy as a youth outreach program. The web-like symbol, a series of concentric circles, refers to the organization's focus on individual improvement through active participation. Typefaces, images, and color reference the Learning Web's commitment to youth, community, growth, and empowerment.

Futura

1

2

the lear**ningweb**

3

4

growth+empowerment

youth+community

youth growth + empowerment

24 anabel taylor hall cornell university ithaca ny 20019 301.636.1236 lwebecornell.edu

The symbol is based on a flexible system capable of transformation into several variations. Its underlying structure includes circular, horizontal, vertical, and diagonal parts. Forms derived from the structure are concentric circles referring to the focus the program puts on individuals. Directional arrows represent growth and change. Images of active youth interact with these elements, establishing a great variety of forms. Three symbol variations are shown here. Used in any combination, the bright primary hues reflect the idealistic spirit of the organization.

1

The design process led to several logotype studies, some of which are presented here.

2

The designated typefaces for the identity program are Futura and Serifa. The geometric shapes of Futura's letters match the circularity of the symbol. Serifa complements Futura, but it also has its own personality. Used in combination, the two typefaces refer to merging learning resources. This detail shows how in the name of the organization the typefaces are combined into a single, uninterrupted unit.

3

The identity allows for a high degree of typographic expression. In details from variations on two letterheads, type overlaps and shoots off at discordant angles. Futura and Serifa carry on their romance, while different sizes and weights of type are juggled to establish infor-mational hierarchy.

4

The figures appearing in the background represent a palette of photos that can be incorporated into the symbol.

youth growth + empowerment

24 anabel taylor hall cornell university ithaca ny 20010 301.656.1236 lweb@cornell.edu

24 anabel taylor hall
cornell university ithaca ny 14835
thelearningweb

353.1482 lweb@aol.com

5

A letterhead, envelope, and business card (front and back), reveal a typographic identity radiating with energy.

the learningweb

youth + community

curtis ogden

Design:
Nancy Nowacek

Client:
The Space for Learning & Doing, a not-for-profit program, offers educational enrichment programs to members of the community. Based on a "community center" idea, the Space provides instruction as well as access to the latest technology.

Concept:
The ampersand separating the two parts of the organization's name, *Learning & Doing,* is the symbol upon which the logotype's design is based. It is an engaging mark consisting of a labyrinth of active shapes connoting the concept of "space". As such, it provides an apt metaphor for the processes of learning and doing.

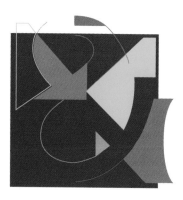

1

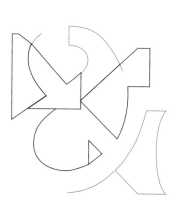

2

3

4

5

5
In an announcement for the organization, a playground of shapes derived from the system projects a lively "learning & doing" environment.

6
Stationery designs reveal the elasticity of the identity system. Note the varied presentation of the logotype.

2
Compare the basic Futura ampersand with the outlined structure developed from this character.

3
A black and white as well as a color variation of the logotype reveal the pliability of the system.

1
The starting point for the design of the logotype is a Futura Regular ampersand. By creating paths of the strokes of the ampersand and the counterforms surrounding it, a framework surfaces. This framework serves as the mark's basic structure and the organizational strategy of the entire identity system. Within the flexible bounds of this system, the logotype changes from application to application. The lines and shapes remain constant, but the designated system colors shift about freely.

4
These are the lines and shapes of a disassembled logotype. They are sometimes used independently within applications to reinforce the "space" theme and to provide consistency.

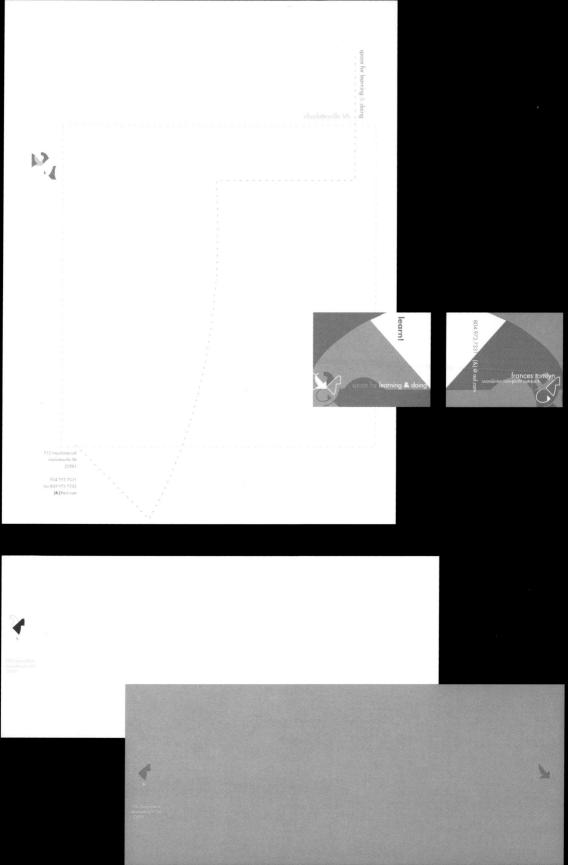

space for learning & doing

charlottesville VA

learn!

space for learning & doing

804.973.7331 [&] @ aol.com

frances tomlyn
coordinator non-profit outreach

510 meadowbrook
charlottesville VA
22901

804 973 7331
fax 804 973 7232
[&] @aol.com

105 maple place
charlottesville, VA
22901

105 maple place
charlottesville, VA
22901

Design:
Amy A. Puglisi

Client:
The Chesapeake Bay Foundation is a non-profit organization with the mission of restoring and sustaining the Chesapeake Bay's ecosystem. The primary roles of the foundation are to influence government, build an environmental ethic, and encourage a love for the Bay, which hopefully encourages people to take action.

Concept:
The identity program reveals the Chesapeake Bay as not simply a body of water, but a complex, ever-changing ecosystem. The circular, interlocking forms composing the logotype signify the circular nature of the ecosystem. This mark may be systematically transformed to represent the Bay's current condition in the areas of water and air quality, land conservation, and animal habitat.

1

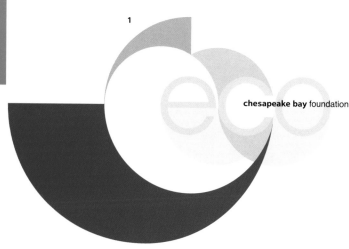

chesapeake bay foundation

2

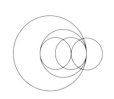

3

4

2
The logotype for the Chesapeake Bay Foundation is built on a circular framework. Nested as the focal point within this structure are the perfectly round letters, *eco*. Blue and its various shades are used to represent the natural environment and the elements water and air.

The interlocking system of circles upon which the logotype design is based.

3
Futura, the font chosen for the identity, is a typeface of pure geometry and balanced proportion. Its circular shapes correspond to the cyclical motions of an ecosystem.

4
During the early stages of the design process, the computer is used to generate "thumbnails." Forms were systematically generated in response to the ecological themes of the Chesapeake Bay.

5

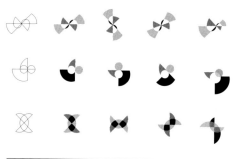

5
Once the circular form for the logotype was determined, it was explored further through various software applications. The use of filters led to fascinating visual possibilities, some of which could be adapted to the identity program. Logotype interpretations shown here allude to such themes as air, water, and pollution.

7

Signage for a kiosk was
developed from variations of
the logotype. The integration
of the signage into the kiosk
is shown in the model to the
right. The smaller model
pictured directly above
reveals how the structure of
the logotype is also the basis
for the kiosk's architecture.

Design:
Amy A. Puglisi

Client:
Legacy, an outreach program led by community volunteers, assists people in organizing and creating a "time capsule," or archival record – beyond simple documentation – for the individual, family, or community. The program helps people to define their unique role in the world and to record an expression of their heritage.

Concept:
The identity for Legacy is built on an interchangeable system of letterforms that metaphorically represent the objects found in a time capsule. The time capsule is a cube-shaped modular container consisting of boxes, shelves, drawers, and other storage units that can be organized and fitted with mementos in any fashion.

1
The fundamental logotype consists of hairline letters based on Futura. Their construction is extremely simple and geometric. The *E*, consisting of only three horizontal strokes, is the most reduced of the letters. An arrow functioning also as the *G* in *Legacy* refers to the cyclical nature of a time capsule – artifacts projected forward in time causing thought and reflection about the past.

2
While the primary logotype always appears on stationery and other business items, several related variations are integrated into applications such as brochures, invitations, and signage. Representatives from the extended logotype family are shown here. A sprightly collection of three-dimensional letters and letters built of lines and planes suggests articles contained within a time capsule.

3
The basic mark appears together with an image of a baby's shoe, an object of deep personal value.

4

5
The arrow, transformed by software filters into an array of textures and gestures, is used in various applications – including the time capsule itself – as a recurring, thematic sign. Photographic images of the sign, such as this one of a scratch in the sand, also adds to the system's vocabulary.

A quotation effectively forms the circular part of the arrow. Type is carefully joined to a circular path.

Inside us are the years we've lived, each wrapped around the last, a layering that makes us all the sum of what is past

6
The time capsule is a transparent structure consisting of box-like modules. It resonates with type and images inserted into slots in the faces, and precious objects placed into the storage spaces.

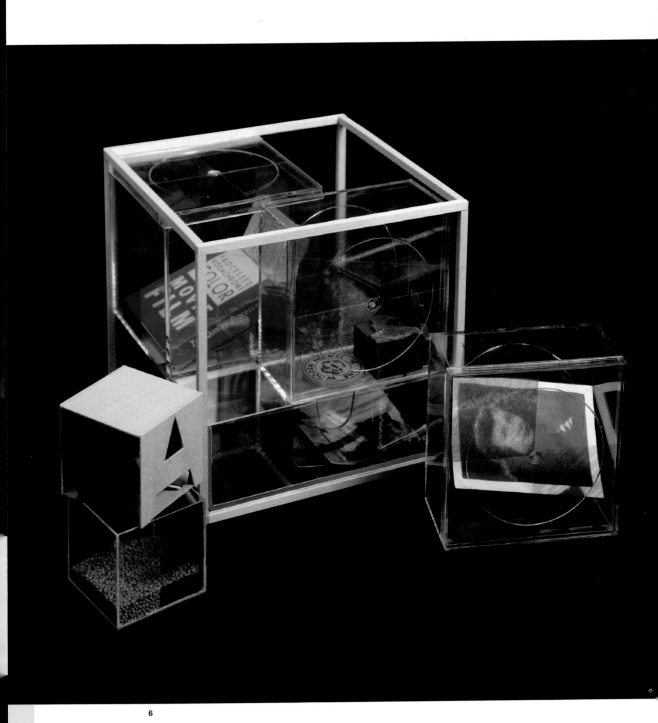

Agri-Couture manufactures a line of biodegradable products and packaging made from cornstarch. From pencils to razors, the primary concern of this environmentally-progressive company is the ecologically-sound disposal of the products.

The logotype and other applications, such as product packaging, reflect the colors, textures, and shapes associated with the corn plant. Packaging material is made from cornstarch, attaining a transparent quality not unlike corn husk. The corn metaphor is carried further with packaging that is opened in much the same way that an ear of corn is "shucked."

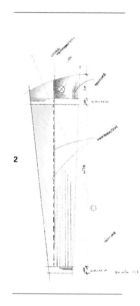

1

2

3

...in that packaging is inherently three-dimensional, models were made to test ideas related to the corn theme. Though very rough, the models helped the designer to converge upon a solution. Here, translucent paper, wire, color, and type suggest an ear of corn. Note the visual similarities between the computer sketches and this model.

The computer proved indispensable when testing color or visualizing specific type effects, such as the organically curved type seen in these early sketches for packaging. Some of the gestural forms, type, and color seen in these studies are incorporated into the final packaging. These studies represent a critical stage in the development of the identity system.

In developing this identity, pencil and computer were both used to articulate thinking and to get ideas into visual form. The pencil was most effective in getting initial thoughts down on paper.

A lyrical composition of shapes based on the design of Gill Sans letters possesses the leafy attributes of the corn plant. The color and transparency created through these overlapping shapes intensify the effect. Contained within the shapes are the letters *a* and *c*, for *Agri-Couture*. Gill Sans possesses subtle organic features, making it an excellent choice for the identity's primary typeface. The shapes composing the logotype also suggest a sickle.

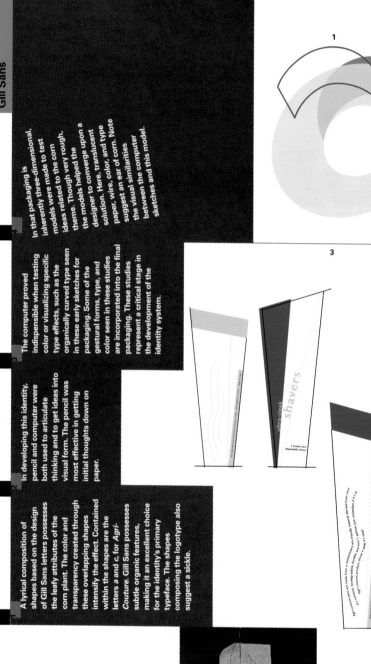

ultra-sleek shavers

pen easy glide

black
x-fine
felt tip
disposable

couture

4

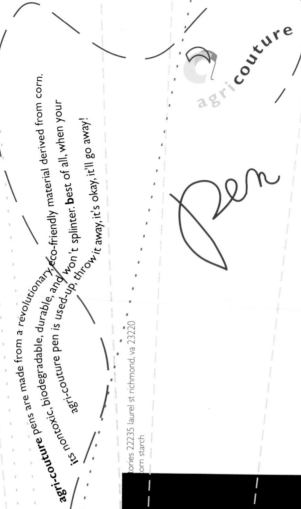

agri couture

Pen

agri-couture pens are made from a revolutionary, biodegradable, durable, eco-friendly material derived from corn.

its nontoxic, biodegradable, and won't splinter. **b**est of all, when your

agri-couture pen is used-up, throw it away, it's okay, it'll go away!

...tories 22235 laurel st richmond, va 23220

...orn starch

5

These animated studies reveal the uninhibited and playful use of the computer to explore design possibilities. This painterly approach seems particularly suited to the identity concept.

Final Agri-Couture packaging integrates the logotype, variations in the use of Gill Sans, botanical color, and frond-like shapes for a highly innovative concept in product packaging.

5

6

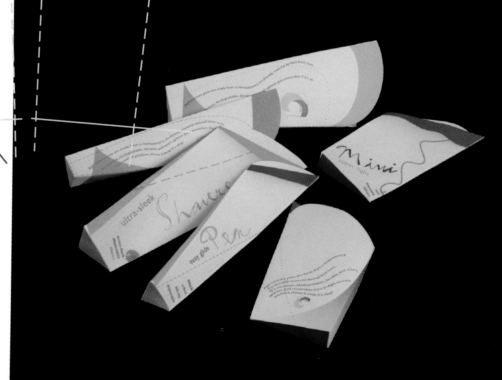

ultra-sleek

Shavere

easy *Pen*

Mini

Design:
Rafael Tr
Jose Lui
TD2, S.E

Design:
David Co

Three interlockin
letters form a
stellation t
moving
Thou
u

The logotype, based on the abbreviated name *MILLERCOMM,* is typeset in a straightforward arrangement of upper-case Helvetica Black Condensed letters. This arrangement is consistently presented in a band running across the top of the poster. Each year, the new season is indicated by a change in the date at the end of the name.

5

EntRAda

FORMS *that soar*

FROM QUIET

SHADED DEPTHS *to* AERIAL

MAJESTY

AND *by their*

GRANDEUR

stir the HEART

and *lift the*

soul

THROUGH FORMS *of*

en CHANTMENT

GATEWAY TO *THE* SPIRIT *of the* ENCHANTED WILDERNESS

EntRAda

GATEWAY TO
THE SPIRIT
OF THE
ENCHANTED
WILDERNESS

EntRAda

EntRAda

GATEWAY TO
THE SPIRIT
OF THE
ENCHANTED
WILDERNESS

GATEWAY TO THE SPIRIT OF THE ENCHANTED WILDERNESS

EntRAda

GATEWAY TO THE SPIRIT OF THE ENCHANTED WILDERNESS

EntRAda

EntRAda

GATEWAY TO THE SPIRIT OF THE ENCHANTED WILDERNESS

EntRAda

EntRAda

EntRAda
GATEWAY TO
THE SPIRIT
OF THE
ENCHANTED
WILDERNESS

THROUGH THE ARTS. THE INSTITUTE'S

ORIGINAL VISIONARY WAS OUR FRIEND

AND MENTOR WARD ROYLANCE.

OUR MISSION

An author, explorer and teach

AS AN ARTS AND

He spent his life sharing his lo

TO FURTHER P

of the Redrock Desert with

Design:
Alan Ball
Altitude, Inc.

Client:
Altitude Product Design and Development Corporation serves the needs of companies or individuals requiring the expertise of a technologically proficient, process-based product design and development firm.

Concept:
Altitude's corporate identity refects the company's proficiency in product development and the innovative spirit and energy brought by the designers to the problem solving process. The entire system refers to avionics instrumentation, and the name *altitude* refers to the imaginative and lofty thinking of the firm.

A L T I T U D E

1

2

3 **Complementing Orator is Meta Caps, which is used as the primary text type. Elements set in this typeface are generously tracked, providing a touch of spaciousness and elegance. In this detail, single letters contained within small red circles identify the telephone**

4 **and fax information. The dots illuminate the space like tiny instrument lights.**

When all of the elements appear together on the letterhead, they are sized and positioned to provide an atmospheric space. The airplane logo (indicated by blue) aligns with the "A." The bottom fold dotted line). Perfect folds every time!

ALTITUDE, INC.
48 GROVE STREET
DAVIS SQUARE
SOMERVILLE, MA
02144

Ⓟ 617 623 7600
Ⓕ 617 623 7755

[ALTITUDE]

1 **The choice of typefaces supports the avionics metaphor. Orator, a geometric and mechanical typeface, is used in combination with four black corner rules. Together, these elements create an image suggesting the type and symbols that might be found on the instrument panel of an airplane.**

2 **Wit is a spicy ingredient used in the identity system as represented by a paper airplane whirling through the firm's air. This icon reveals the tongue-in-cheek humor and creativity.**

ALTITUDE, INC.
48 GROVE STREET
DAVIS SQUARE
SOMERVILLE, MA
02144

Ⓟ 617 623 7600
Ⓕ 617 623 7755

4

Cheryl Brzezinski-
Beckett
Minor Design Group

The Contemporary Arts Museum of Houston is one of the leading museums in the United States. Its mission is "presenting and interpreting – the art of our time – art as it evolves, art of the present and immediate past."

A wedge of corrugated aluminum on the Houston landscape, the museum is a monument to the art of our time. The museum's visual identity program metaphorically suggests the formal vigor of the architecture as well as the museum's educational mission.

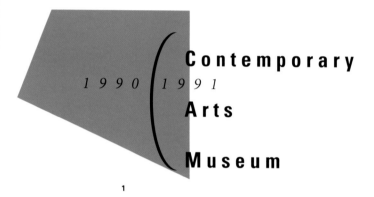

1990 1991

Contemporary

Arts

Museum

1

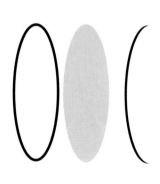

2

1990 1991

Contemporary

Arts

Museum

3

5216 Montrose at Bissonnet
Houston, Texas 77006-6598

713.526.0773

4

5. The logotype is capable of subtle transformation. Compare uses of the logotype in the applications presented (facing page).

4. A small square is used throughout the identity to stress important information such as the address on the envelope. On the letterhead it is used together with a stair-step ruled line to isolate and separate pertinent information. Devices of this kind are referred to as typographic punctuation. Minion serves elegantly as the text for the address block.

2. The bracket used to isolate and emphasize the name of the museum is simply a white oval placed over a black oval. This crescent shape clearly distinguishes the name of the museum as the most important unit of information.

1. The logotype, upbeat and astir with shapes, lines, and types, expresses the museum's essential purpose. A large trapezoid slicing through the name of the museum is the identity's primary motif. This shape along with other distinct elements projects a feeling of modernity. As a whole, this grouping of elements is called a typographic constellation.

3. On the letterhead, the logotype is combined with a curving photograph of corrugated aluminum, a reference to the museum's architecture. The photo-graph's shape complements the logotype's modernity.

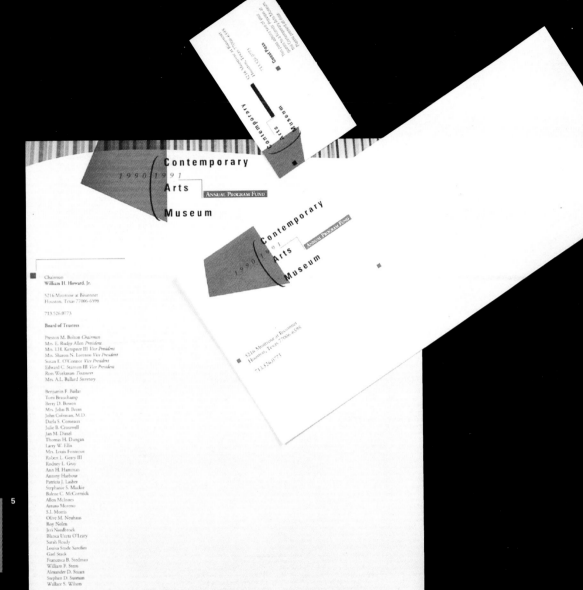

Contemporary
1990 / 1991
Arts
Museum

ANNUAL PROGRAM FUND

April Greiman
Greimanski Labs

Nicola is a restaurant serving the needs of patrons within the Los Angeles area. Located in the Sanwa Bank Building, the restaurant serves a large Asian population.

Referring to the visual textures and tones of the restaurant environment, images of wood and stone combine with coded typographic identifiers and color for a varied and rich identity program.

n

o

m
b   g   l
          e   u   r
        v
          d

1

2

The primary typeface of the identity is Modula, a sleek, highly condensed typeface with a pronounced verticality. A characteristic of its design is the peculiarly angled strokes of characters such as the lower-case *i*, *n*, and *g*. This affectation provides the letters with a quality slightly reminiscent of Japanese characters.

The identity is composed of a mixture of typographic forms, textural photographs, circles and squares, and a color palette of distinctive hues: green, violet, and red. These elements appear from application to application in great variety. On occasion, *NICOLA* appears as a vertical strip of paired letters. This serves as a visual pun for Kanji characters. The *N* for Nicola is usually (but not always) found in a circle as in the *M* in metro stop signage. This letter belongs to Futura. Restaurant paraphernalia exhibit the visual variety achieved by these elements.

The square is a fundamental motif of the identity, providing a basic structure for the business card and other items. Front and back views of the business card are shown here, along with other stationery components.

a

NICOLA

600 S Figueroa
Los Angeles
California 90017
213 461 0427
213 461 0439 FAX

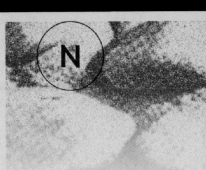

Design:
Carlos Segura
Segura Inc.

Photography:
Eric Dinyer

Client:
Waxtrax!/TVT Records specializes in alternative rock, techno-industrial, and rap music. Bands featured by the label include Ministry, Revolting Cocks, KMFDM, Life with the Thrill Kill Cult, and Coil.

Concept:
When Waxtrax Records restructured, having been purchased by TVT Records in New York, the only thing left of this metaphorical plane crash was a "black box" containing a three-CD compilation set containing 41 songs. Segura created an identity for the packaging which chronicles an entire genre of music.

2

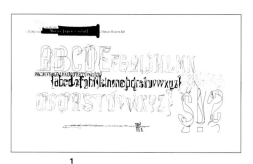

1

1 The twisted, molten name of the CD sampler, *Black Box*, is typeset in Moire, a typeface designed by Harriet R. Goren. Moire may be lumped into an expressive genre of typeface design that developed as a result of the Macintosh revolution. There is nothing conventional about the face; it is not intended to be readable in the traditional sense. It does, however, evoke a reader's emotional response. As much image as it is word, this wild typeface is felt as well as read.

3

2 Set in two sizes of the open (outline) version of Moire, the logotype looks like wire, bent and mangled into letterforms. Letters in the name *Black Box* are wrapped together by tentative, meandering horizontal lines. The whole structure may fall apart at any time.

The identity's secondary typeface is Tema Cantante by Eric Lin. An expressive face with sharp, gothic features, it is used for text.

3 In keeping to the black box theme, the color black dominates the various applications, providing a dark resonance. Illustrations rendered in warm, golden hues provide startling contrast. These images, richly symbolic, connote an alternative music subculture.

4 The Black Box collection comes in several different sets. A limited edition set, packaged in an industrial-strength black box covered with wire mesh, contains the CDs, a poster, party coasters, an embroidered patch, and a 72-page book.

Paula Scher
Ron Louie
Lisa Mazur
Pentagram Design Inc.

The Public Theater is recognized as one of New York City's leading venues for new theatrical productions. It is perhaps best known for its annual summer production of the New York Shakespeare Festival in Central Park.

Referring to the typography and graffiti of the street, the spirited identity program for The Public Theater utilizes a variety of wood typefaces. These typefaces, in their great variety, work harmoniously to demand attention and to entertain the eye. Round, monogrammed stamps represent each of the individual theaters within The Public.

1

THE PUBLIC THEATER

2

6

3

1
Designed from a variety of wood types, including Morgan Gothic, the logotype forms a compact, rectangular unit. The descending widths and weights of the letters move the eye to the word *THEATER,* which is aligned with the height of the capital letters in the word *PUBLIC.*

2–4
For announcements and advertisements, a potpourri of wood types from the nineteenth century democratically bristle against each other in a way that is both elegant and edgy. Individual events are compartmentalized into textural typographic fields that are adaptable to various allotments of ad space. The visual shimmer of the wood types extends into promotional items such as t-shirts as well.

5
Each of the individual theaters within The Public Theater is identified by a distinctive monogram (a design composed of one or more letters, usually the initials of a name).

6
A photograph of the interior of a theater reveals the application of the logotype, monograms, and signage designed from wood type.

5

THEATER
PUBLIC
THE

— 435 Lafayette Street, New York, NY 10003

BLADE, TO THE HEAT

By Oliver Mayer • Directed by George C. White
Starts October 10 • The game: boxing.
The stakes: light in the ring and on the line—
machismo vs. a new sexual terrain. An arresting new play set
in the Latin boxing world of the late 1950's.

THEATER
PUBLIC '95
THE

'94 WAYS TO GET IN ON
THE GROUND FLOOR.
AND EASY NEW
BRAVE NEW WORLDS
BRAVE NEW WORKS,
THE

THE DIVA
IS DISMISSED

Written and Performed by Jenifer Lewis • Directed by Charles Randolph-Wright
October 27 - November 13 The repertory wits "Don't People"! - the New York Times
christened her "Diva Queen of Coca's Cabaret"—and now she's having that Life and
working it. Triple-threat comedienne/actress/vocalist Jenifer Lewis takes us on a
ribald, rockets and heart-wrenching journey through her life and times.

PEOPLE
SOME PEOPLE

Written and Performed by Danny Hoch • Directed by Jo Bonney • October 14 - November 13
(Extended run)

A New Musical • Book by Edward Gallardo
Music & Lyrics by Michael John LaChiusa
Choreographed by Rob Marshall • Starts December 3

THE PETRIFIED PRINCE

"Could a petrified, neurotic, schizophrenic, catatonic, uncommunicative cretin become King?"
A ribald new musical, based on an original screenplay by Ingmar Bergman.

SIMPATICO

Written and Directed by Sam Shepard • Starts November 5 • Sam Shepard returns to The Public with
a high-stakes look at the dirty-double-dealings of two horseracing businessmen. The field features
Beverly D'Angelo, James Gammon, Marcia Gay Harden, Ed Harris, Fred Ward and Welker White.

THE MERCHANT OF VENICE

By William Shakespeare • Directed by Barry Edelstein
Starts January 17 • In 1954, a church basement on the Lower
East Side of Manhattan, Joseph Papp presented the first production
of what was to become known, the world over, as The New York
Shakespeare Festival. And so we celebrate our 40th Anniversary, as
Tony-winner Ron Leibman ("Angels in America") exacts a pound of
flesh, and the Shakespeare Marathon continues.

HIM

By Christopher Walken • Reunited by Tim Supple •

SILENCE, CUNNING, EXILE

By Stuart Greenman
Directed by Mark Wing-Davey • February
America, circa 1955. He is an intellectual's
son out. So Sadie, Daniel, Beryl and Frank
flee to Martha's Vineyard, where bohemia
beckons amid madness descends. A play
suggested by the life of Diane Arbus.

LANGUAGE
OF THEIR OWN
A

By Clay Yew • January •

DOG OPERA

By Constance Congdon • Directed by Gerald Gutierrez • April
They kibitz about their thighs...laugh at the same jokes...share the
same neuroses. They'd probably be married...if one of them weren't a
guy. Peter and Madeline—two people desperate to find "a lover what
they've already found in each other. A contemporary comedy about
life, love and loneliness in the '90s.

ON MOONLIGHT
DANCING

By Keith Grant • March

JOIN

Design:
Matt Woolman

Client:
The Center for Design Studies, a think tank for design at Virginia Commonwealth University, provides a forum for the exchange of ideas about the future of design and the effect of new technology on the profession. *Zed,* the Center's journal, is published annually.

Concept:
The idea for the logotype comes from circuit diagrams found on computer chips. Emerging from the circuits are the letters *CDS* for Center for Design Studies. The fin-like shape containing the circuits stirs a nostalgic stew of post-WWII futuristic motifs. We are perhaps reminded of a Jetson cartoon.

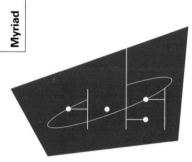

1

2

3

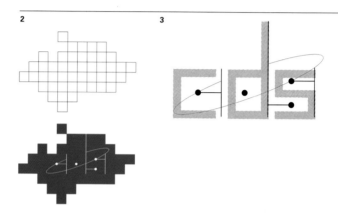

virginia commonwealth university

communication arts + design
325 north harrison street
richmond, virginia 23284-2519

voice 804.828.1709
fax 804.828.6469

5

center for design studies

center for design studies

center for design studies

center for design studies

center for design studies

4

1
Contained within the 1950s futuristic shape, dots and lines representing computer circuitry form the letters *cds* for Center for Design Studies. The ellipse suggests a molecular structure. The color purple was chosen because it is not too serious nor too wacky.

2
A grid was used for the design of the logotype. The diagrams reveal how the logotype was constructed using this tool.

3
For those having difficulty seeing the letters cds in the logotype, this diagram reveals their presence. The letters are indicated in gray.

4
A palette of logotype possibilities was developed for incorporation into different applications. These include variations in color and elaborations of the standard logotype.

5
All parts of the identity share some relationship with other parts. In this detail of the business card, type is angled to relate to the logotype's purple shape. Myriad functions as the identity's primary typeface. Possessing both humanistic and geometric qualities, it acknowledges the organization's concern for both humanity and technology.

center for design studies
MAX BILL

center for design studies
MAX BILL

• virginia commonwealth university

communication arts + design
325 north harrison street
richmond, virginia 23284-2519

voice 804.828.1709
fax 804.828.6469

www http://128.172.172.6/.SOTASERVER/CDEHomepage/CDE.html

•

virginia commonwealth university

communication arts + design
325 north harrison street
richmond, virginia 23284-2519

voice 804.828.1709   **fax** 804.828.6469   **www** http://128.172.172.6/.SOTASERVER/CDEHomepage/CDE.html

6

**Stationery reveals the vitality
and energy of the identity
system.**

virginia commonwealth university

communication arts + design
325 north harrison street
richmond, virginia 23284-2519

Carlos Segura
Segura Inc.

Photography:
Photonica

How magazine, a bi-monthly publication, features case studies on techniques, processes, and ideas of graphic design, typography, illustration, photography, and animation.

Each year, *How* magazine sponsors a design conference. In creating an identity for the 1993 event, which carried the theme "Creative Vision," Carlos Segura focused on the ideas of experimentation and seeing old things in a new way. Neo, a typeface designed by Segura and used for the logotype, combines influences from various sources to create a new blend.

Neo

1
The identity consists of two primary elements: the word *how,* and the theme of the conference, *creative vision. how* is typeset in Neo, a typeface designed by Carlos Segura. Because the three letters composing the word are highly unusual in form (the *W* is one of the oddest letters in the font), the unit serves as a distinct center-piece for the identity. *Creative Vision* is typeset in Keedy, a funky typeface with round, square, and diagonal terminals; the dot of the *i* is curiously small. A third typeface used in the identity is the quirky Template Gothic.

2
Neo combines both serif and sans serif features. This gives the font an indeterminate, ambiguous quality, and a rare charm. At first glance the face might actually appear as foreign characters, perhaps Cyrillic.

3
The experimental zeal of the designer is realized in the many different expressions of the logotype. For the conference registration form, *how* appears blurred, having been taken through computer filters. *creative vision* is centered over this element and printed in red.

4
An announcement combines the theme of the conference, *Creative Vision,* with one of several illustrations suggesting creativity. On the back of the announcement, a menagerie of active type forces reader attention.

5
Announcements and registration forms express the dynamics of creativity.

1

how creative vision

The 1993 **How Design Conference** on Business and The Creative Process, April 25th thru 28th, 1993, The Westin Hotel, Chicago, Illinois.

2

AabbCDEFGHI iJKKhLMmnhn OPPPOQrSTT UUVIHXYYZ

+1234567890/

3

4

creative vision

HOW The 1993 HOW DESIGN CONFERENCE on Business and The Creative Process. April 25th thru 28th, 1993, The Westin Hotel, Chicago, Illinois.

Don't miss out!
Registration deadline is April 2nd

PAID

Experience the exploration of creative vision in CHICAGO. Plan now to attend the one conference that focuses on both the BUSINESS AND CREATIVE aspects of design.

The 1993 HOW DESIGN CONFERENCE

Call TOLL FREE **800. 666. 0963** or 513.531.2222.

creative vision

HOW The 1993 How Design Conference on Business and The Creative Process.
April 25th thru 28th, 1993. The Westin Hotel, Chicago, Illinois.

Design:
April Greiman
Greimanski Labs

Illustration:
Neal Izumi
Michael Rotondi
Lorna Turner
April Greiman

Client:
Greimanski Labs, a collaborative design studio located in Los Angeles, engages in print, environmental and architectural graphic design, and video. Staff designers use the computer as a conceptual as well as a production tool. The principal designer, April Greiman, has a reputation for her cutting-edge experimentation.

Concept:
April Greiman describes the concept of her visual identity program as "the Greimanski self-correcting mainframe on fire." The image representing this tongue-in-cheek concept may be found in multiple permutations in the stationery system. The conceptual reference to computers is supported by the use of the typeface OCR-A.

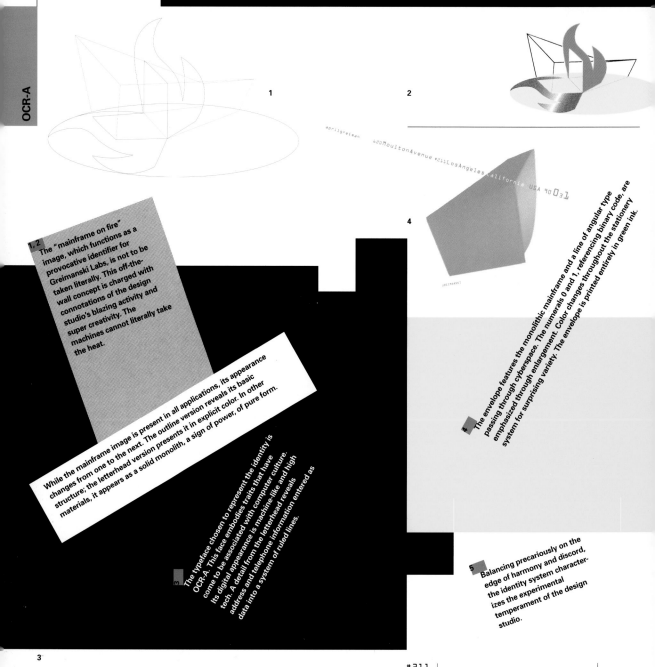

1

2

4

1, 2
The "mainframe on fire" image, which functions as a provocative identifier for Greimanski Labs, is not to be taken literally. This off-the-wall concept is charged with connotations of the design studio's blazing activity and super creativity. The machines cannot literally take the heat.

While the mainframe image is present in all applications, its appearance changes from one to the next. The outline version reveals its basic structure; the letterhead version presents it in explicit color. In other materials, it appears as a solid monolith, a sign of power, of pure form.

3
The typeface chosen to represent the identity is OCR-A. This face embodies traits that have come to be associated with computer culture. Its digital appearance is machine-like and high tech. A detail from the letterhead reveals address and telephone information entered as data into a system of ruled lines.

4
The envelope features the monolithic mainframe and a line of angular type passing through cyberspace. The numerals 0 and 1, referencing binary code, are emphasized through enlargement. Color changes throughout the stationery system for surprising variety. The envelope is printed entirely in green ink.

5
Balancing precariously on the edge of harmony and discord, the identity system characterizes the experimental temperament of the design studio.

3

```
Greimanski        620 Moulton Ave    #211    Los Angeles
Apriliska                              USA   (213)
                  California 90031            227 1 2 2 2
                                             (213)    fax
                                             227 8 6 5 1
```

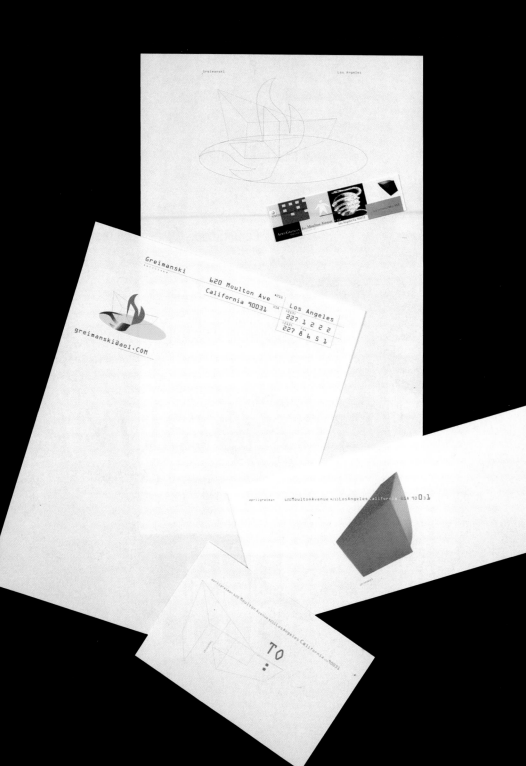

A carefully administered identity program insures that every aspect of a company's image meets required design standards. These areas include signage, vehicular graphics, advertising and marketing, and internal corporate communications. The General Instrument identity materials presented here reveal a high degree of quality and consistency.

6

7

8

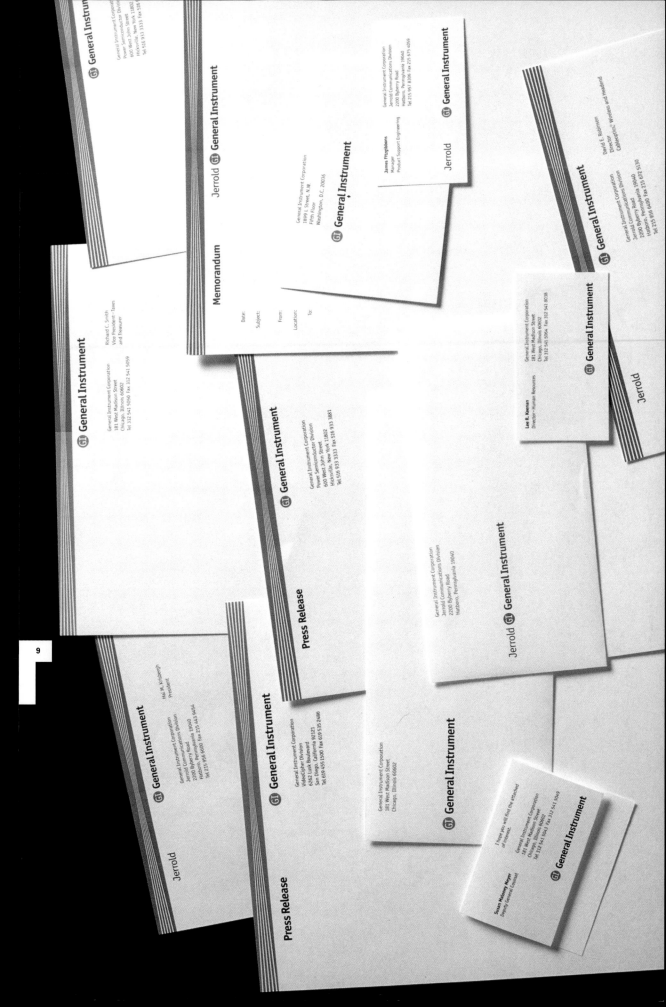

Design:
Jen Bracy

Client:
Meridian, a women's international travel organization, provides a travel network whereby women are matched with other women and furnished with information to ensure safe international travel.

Concept:
A curvilinear Oxford *m* is cradled within two overlapping circles representing a globe of the world. The mark prompts other travel associations as well, including latitude and longitude lines, a compass, and a weather vane indicating the four cardinal directions.

3

meridian   **meridian**

Oxford

1

2

meridian

meridian

4

The Oxford lower-case *m*, for *Meridian*, corresponds in shape to the circles of a globe. The overlap of the two circles aligns exactly to the curves of the letter for a perfect fit.

Oxford is a calligraphic face that resembles Caroline minuscules, a standard form of handwriting used during the eighth to the twelfth centuries. This medieval period is strongly associated with maritime travel.

For flexibility, two versions of the logotype were designed. The first is reversed from a solid square to appear as white. The second logotype, free from the square, suggests a spinning globe. Both versions are presented in either black or blue (the specific shade of blue is a color often associated with international travel signs). The name *Meridian*, which may or may not accompany the logotype, is set in Garamond Italic. This typeface shares the curvilinear traits of the logotype and may shift in position from application to application.

Preliminary research for the identity includes a study of the word *meridian* as it appears in different typefaces. The structure and rhythmic patterns of the word were explored by means of lines and circles. The lines began to suggest latitude and longitude lines, the circles a globe. Using the computer to freely explore the attributes of type can lead to ideas and inspiration. Presented here is just a small sampling of these studies.

Stationery shows the system at work. Layout is based on a grid of squares related to the logotype. Several carefully placed logotypes, screened to a very light value, suggest points on a map. Signage takes on the appearance of a weather vane (facing page).

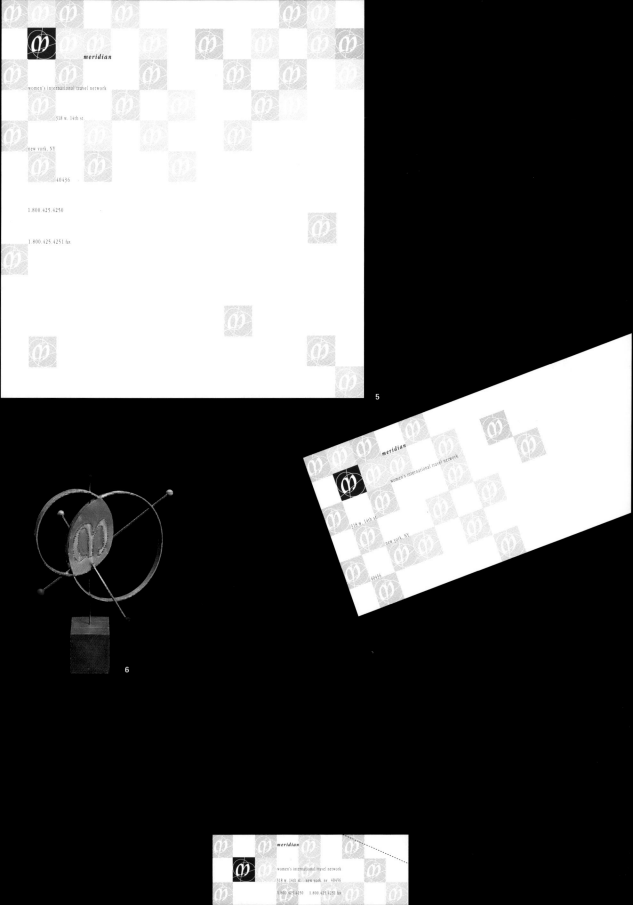

meridian

women's international travel network

318 w. 14th st.

new york, NY

40436

1.800.425.4250

1.800.425.4251 fax

5

6

Design:
April Greiman

Photography:
AG/Justin Siegel

Illustration:
April Greiman

Client:
Lux Pictures, guided by producers James Magowan and Martin Kistler, engages in a variety of motion picture projects, including the comedy *Impossible* and the dark comedy *Flesh Suitcase*.

Concept:
The identity program is based on Syntax, a clean, energetic typeface that avoids the typical look of Hollywood nostalgia. A rectangle referencing a movie screen with a gradation of color representing light forms a backdrop for animated letters that shift about from one application to another.

L U X

1

a a a a a a a a a a

2

3

PICTURES U X

PICTURES U X
L

4

Syntax, the typeface used in this identity, is clean and friendly, and youthful in appearance. The letters *L, U,* and *X,* representing the name of the film company, animate the space like actors on a screen. The *X* is the most exuberant of the three letters. In the film context, this letter can easily be read as a pictographic figure with out-stretched arms. The character traits of Syntax are key to the effectiveness of the identity, but the calculated scaling and placement of the letters is equally important.

Some letters are serious, others humorous; some are quiet and easygoing, others loud and obnoxious. It is a letter's inherent shape and proportion that separates it from others, makes it unique. Designers tuned in to the personalities of typefaces (which are often very subtle) can take advantage of them when tackling typographic problems.

The logotype is presented in two ways: reversed from a rectangle of blended color to appear as white, and printed as red and black letters on a light background. Integrating the letters into the gradational rectangle generates a dramatic effect.

The word *PICTURES* provides a delicate counterpoint to the more emphatic *LUX.* Its small size adds to the pictorial essence of the configuration, appearing off in the distance.

The stationery exhibits other important design features. Relating to the deliberate horizontal movement of the word *PICTURES,* thin ruled lines divide information blocks.

The slight variance in design from one stationery component to another provides the identity with visual vitality (facing page).

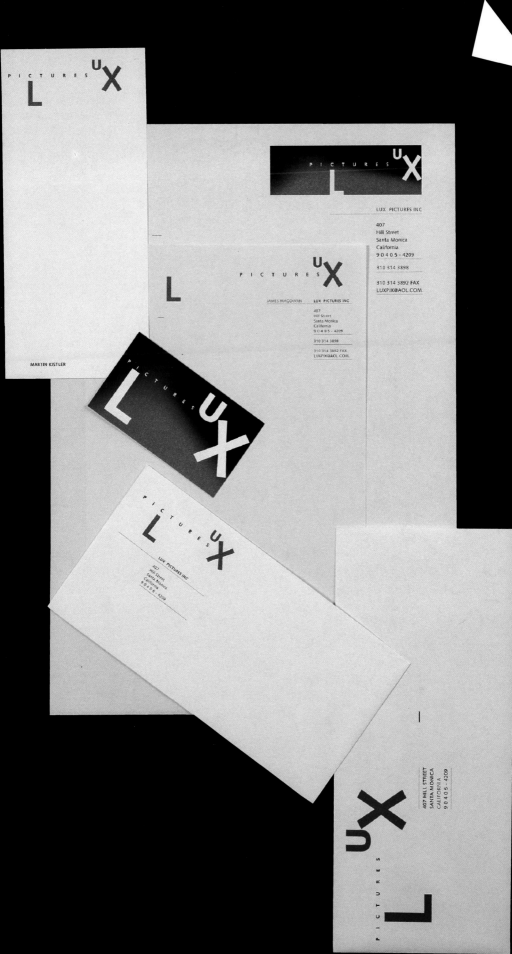

Matt Woolman

The Germ Press is a small publishing company specializing in contemporary hypertext literature and high-end collectors' editions of out-of-print books.

The company takes its name from the meaning in "germ" or "germinate": something that may serve as the basis for further knowledge and growth. Visually, the logotype represents this process. It also refers to the company's mission of pursuing traditional quality bookmaking while keeping one foot in the future.

Syntax

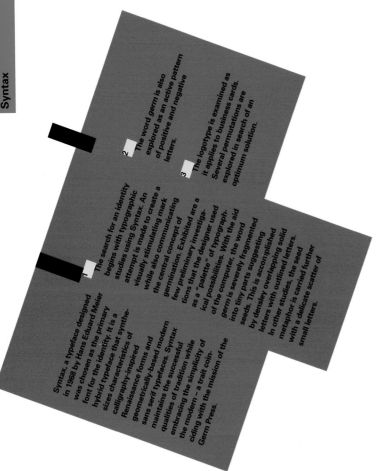

Syntax, a typeface designed in 1968 by Hans Eduard Meier was chosen as the primary font for the identity. It is a hybrid typeface that synthesizes characteristics of calligraphy-inspired Renaissance forms and geometrically-based modern sans serif typefaces. Syntax maintains the successful qualities of tradition while embracing the simplicity of the modern – a trait coinciding with the mission of the Germ Press.

1 The search for an identity begins with typographic studies using Syntax. An attempt is made to create a visually stimulating mark while also communicating the central concept of germination. Exhibited are a few preliminary investigations that the designer used as a "palette" of typographical possibilities. With the aid of the computer, the word germ is severely fragmented into tiny parts suggesting by densley overlapping solid letters with outlined letters. In other studies, the seed metaphor is carried further with a delicate scatter of small letters.

2 The word germ is also explored as an active pattern of positive and negative letters.

3 The logotype is examined as it applies to business cards. Several permutations are explored in search of an optimum solution.

3

2

1

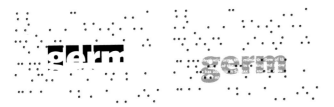

germ **PRESS**

b   s   o

k   c

a

t

v

l

n

x

q

z

f   u   p

y

i   w   h   j

3133   connecticut   avenue
northwest, suite   730
washington,   d.c.   20008
voice 202.797.0761
online eszett@aol.com

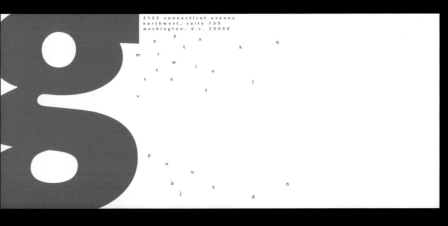

3133 connecticut avenue
northwest, suite 730
washington, d.c. 20008

e   y   x

m   r   t   k   q

s   w   i

c   a   n

v   f   l

p

o

u

b   z   h

j

d

The final stationery system
exhibits a synthesis of the
ideas generated in
preliminary identity studies.
The varied implementation of
identity elements, such as the
enlargement of the g for the
envelope and the use of a
solid red background for the
business card, provides a
____ant countenance.

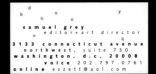

germ PRESS

w   f   l   x

s   a   t   x   j

v   k   p   z

b   d   h   y

b   h   n

samuel grey
editor+art director
u   q

3133 connecticut avenue
northwest, suite 730
washington, d.c. 20008
voice 202.797.0761
online eszett@aol.com

Design:
Carlos Segura
Segura Inc.

Illustration:
Tony Klassen
Carlos Segura

Client:
[T-26], a new digital type foundry based in Chicago, promotes typographic experimentation, and the type designs of both students and professionals. The company caters to the needs of designers, art directors or anyone with a computer.

Concept:
The sundry materials encompassing the identity system for [T-26] include type catalogs, samples showing new typefaces, and a potpourri of other promotional materials. These are all contained inside of a Font Kit, a cloth bag otherwise known as a "T-bag."

The identity for this type foundry is driven by experimental fervor. Type specimen catalogs, announcements, advertisements, and all other materials associated with the foundry exhibit kinetic vibrance and an untamed visual resonance. There is nothing traditional about [T-26] – not in the library of typefaces and other offerings by the foundry, nor in the image projected by the company's diverse identity.

1
The primary font used in the identity is Tema Cantante by Eric Lin. Shown here are specimens of this typeface from the type catalog. These catalog pages not only provide a sense of the alternative type library offered by the foundry; they also reveal one of the identity's essential qualities: a certain honest rawness tempered by sophistication and elegance.

2
Shown in a detail from a catalog page, a curious decorative shape contains the font name, type designer, and price. Motifs such as this are common to the identity, providing an element of visual distinction.

3
The logotype is the name [T-26] set in Tema Cantante. This mark is supported by another recurring typographical form: an outline of a three-dimensional *T*. Referencing computers and digital type, this motif often appears as a mirror image. This treatment of the mark provides spatial depth, and it dramatizes the bi-lateral symmetry of the page layouts. Shown in these examples is a representative sampling of anouncements.

4
Contents of the Font Kit, including font catalogs, announcements of new typefaces, posters, and other knick knacks related to [T-26].

1

2

3

4

5

Design:
David Colley

Client:
SEAMUS is a nonprofit organization of composers, performers, and teachers of electro-acoustic music representing every musical style. The organization promotes concerts and radio broadcasts of electro-acoustic music throughout the world.

Concept:
Presenting a consistent image for this series of recording releases is achieved by repeating the same visual elements on each compact disk while providing some variation through color. The dots refer to "electronic" while the lines signify "acoustic."

1

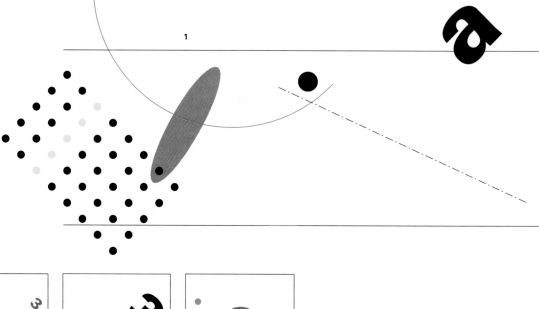

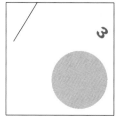  

2

3

Dots, lines, arcs, circles, and swirls are typographic support elements that can be used in concert with letterforms to effectively communicate ideas and to aid the organization of information. In this series of CDs, repeated dots and lines become the visual equivalent of musical sounds. Identical use of these elements from CD to CD provides visual unity. Dynamic rhythmic patterns and textures can be achieved by repeating elements in different ways.

Visual hierarchy is a tool used by designers to help readers distinguish various parts of information. The strategic use of design variables such as scale, color, angle, and position help to establish visual hierarchy. In this identity system, the number of each CD is identified as the main element due to its size, angled placement, and color. The eye then moves to the title of the CD, which is type reversed from a stair-step shape to appear as white. Lastly, the names of the performers – presented in small type as a list – are read. In the diagram, each scenario presents the numeral 3 as the dominant element in the hierarchy.

Stair-step shapes effectively structure and accentuate the titles. Parts of each title are strategically positioned to ensure clearly distinguished roles. The background shape emphasizes this planned organization, providing a spatial compartment for each line of type.

THE SOCIETY FOR ELECTRO-ACOUSTIC MUSIC IN THE UNITED STATES

Music from SEAMUS EAM-9301

James Mobberley

Judith Shatin

Ann Rubin

Stephen Dival Brier

Bernard Iontolius

Kwok and John Cooc

THE SOCIETY FOR ELECTRO-ACOUSTIC MUSIC IN THE UNITED STATES

Music from SEAMUS EAM-9401

Scott A. Wyatt

Jeffrey Hass

Barry Schrader

Cort Lippe

Charles Norman Mason

Salvatore Trifal

James Whitcaney

THE SOCIETY FOR ELECTRO-ACOUSTIC MUSIC IN THE UNITED STATES

Music from SEAMUS EAM-9402

Larry Nelson

Scott A. Wyatt

Joseph Koykkar

Joseph L. Anderson

Charles Norman Mason

Stephen David Beck

Eric David Chasalow

Paul Koonce

...ign:
Communication
Design, Inc.

Client:
Bond, Comet, Westmoreland, and Hiner is an architectural design firm with a strong reputation for innovative problem solving. The firm's work, respectful of the natural and manmade environments, possesses a unique personality and a contemporary flair. Much of the firm's work is in the area of school design.

Concept:
The identity system consists of three elements: the word *architects,* the firm's name, and an arc. The configuration of these three elements changes with each application, suggesting the forward-thinking nature and adaptability of the firm. A consistent element is the arc, a clever visual pun referring to *arc* in the word *architects.*

BOND
COMET
WESTMORELAND
+ HINER

1

**BOND
COMET
WESTMORELAND
+ HINER**

1 Multiple typefaces are used in the identity program. Univers 67 is used for the firm's name for visual as well as practical reasons. It is a bold typeface that holds up well when printed at small sizes; and because it is a narrow face, it minimizes the length of *Westmoreland.* A distinctive, asymmetrical shape is formed by the extension of this word to the right, and the use of the + sign to the left (indicated by the black dotted line, right).

2 To reinforce the kinetic nature of the identity, the firm's name changes color in most applications. The arc is most frequently yellow to maintain a subtle yet active presence. *Architects* is always printed in a warm, light gray to correspond with the conservative treatment of the word, and to avoid conflict with other typographic elements. This reproduction of the letterhead reveals the distribution of the color and one organizational strategy for the elements.

ARCHITECTS

3

2

BOND
COMET
WESTMORELAND
+ HINER

ARCHITECTS

3 *Architects* is set in all-capitals Caslon. Having an established look, this elegant typeface emits a message about the firm's status in the profession. By orienting the word vertically, it assumes the appearance of a built object, functioning as a metaphor for building.

The thin arc begins in the center of the *c* and extends to a point that aligns with the *s* in *architects*. This dynamic, "architectural" element animates the space for a memorable image.

BOND COMET WESTMORELAND + HINER

207 West Broad Street
Richmond, Virginia 23220

ARCHITECTS

BOND COMET WESTMORELAND + HINER

207 West Broad Street
Richmond, Virginia 23220

ARCHITECTS

Sanford Bond, AIA

207 West Broad Street
Richmond, Virginia 23220

804/788-4774 FAX 788-0986

BOND COMET WESTMORELAND + HINER

ARCHITECTS

BOND COMET WESTMORELAND + HINER

207 West Broad Street
Richmond, Virginia 23220

BOND COMET WESTMORELAND + HINER

ARCHITECTS

BOND COMET WESTMORELAND + HINER

804/788-4774 FAX 788-0986

ARCHITECTS

Sanford Bond, AIA
Robert E. Comet, Jr., AIA
Douglas D. Westmoreland, AIA
Henry L. Hiner, AIA

Gordon H. Columbo, AIA (retired)
Fred W. Needham, AIA (retired)
Kenneth G. MacInroy, AIA (deceased)

207 West Broad Street
Richmond, Virginia 23220

804/788-4774 FAX **788-0986**

ARCHITECTS

BOND COMET WESTMORELAND + HINER

207 West Broad Street
Richmond, Virginia 23220

ARCHITECTS

Wanderlust, Inc., is a charter sailboat company consisting of one boat and a crew. The boat sails continuously around the globe as passengers book tours from port to port. The company caters to wealthy clients with adventurous, wandering instincts, but clients who also hope and pray for fair weather.

The problem for the designer was to reveal sailing as an exciting, safe, and very pleasant means of travel. This was achieved by combining recognizable sailboat and sun motifs. Depending on specific applications, the logotype is presented in a palette of bright colors associated with the sailing vernacular.

1

ph: 315 . 475 . 9725

wanderlust, inc.

1001 Westcott Street, Syracuse, NY 13210

wanderlust, inc.

1001 Westcott Street, Syracuse, NY 13210

2

The logotype design is a witty combination of a bold circle signifying the sun and two white triangular shapes representing a sailboat. As if imprinted upon the sail, a lower-case Univers 65 w identifies the sailing company. The triangular counterforms of the w fortuitously correspond to the sail and hull shapes in the logotype, establishing visual unity. Another effective touch is the ruled lined beneath the w. As the only horizontal element in the logotype, it provides a distinctive contrast.

The reliability and flexibility of Univers make it an excellent choice for the system's primary typeface. The simple shapes composing the letters complement the basic geometry of the logotype.

4

3

2

In these details from the letterhead and a business card, lines of type mimic the energetic angles of the logotype. This active dialogue between typographic parts is a quality that ties the various printed applications together and unifies the entire identity system.

3

This is a second, more representational variation of the logotype. The sun motif appears as an outline rather than a solid shape. This simple change, easily made on a computer, dramatically alters the logotype's appearance and provides the identity system with visual variety.

As is true of many great logotype designs, this one appears deceptively simple. It is merely a combination of three elemental shapes. However, for optimum readability, these shapes must be painstakingly sized and positioned.

4

The fixed color palette for the logotype and application typography consists of bright hues of matching intensity.

Debbie Shmerel

Pillars is a company specializing in the design and manufacture of totem-like heirlooms for individuals and families desiring an organized means of storing and preserving family photographs and mementos.

Visually, the logotype suggests a totem pole, and in the context of family, it is a symbol of support and trust. The identity system is highly flexible with the logotype changing for each application. The simplicity and variety of the Univers family provide the qualities necessary to achieve the visual appearance and dynamics of totem poles.

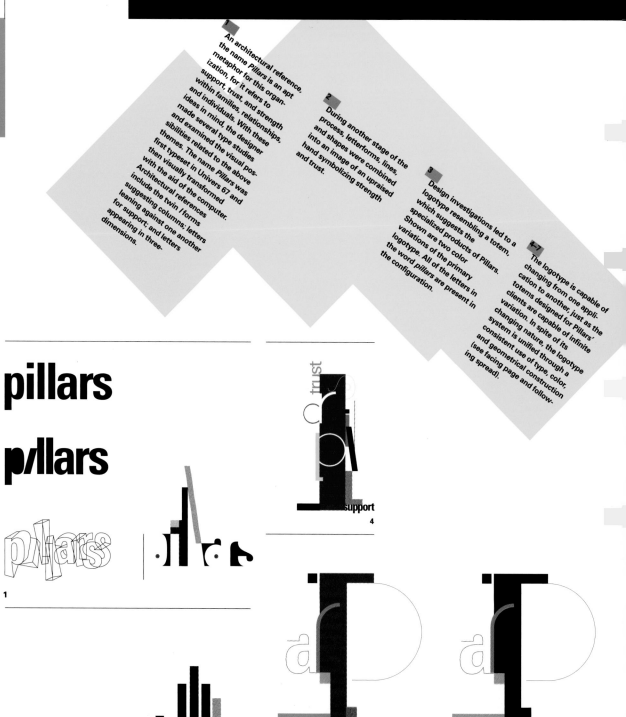

1 An architectural reference, the name *Pillars* is an apt metaphor for this organization, for it refers to support, trust, and strength within families, relationships, and individuals. With these ideas in mind, the designer made several type studies and examined the visual possibilities related to the above themes. The name *Pillars* was first typeset in Univers 67 and then visually transformed with the aid of the computer. Architectural references include the twin *l* forms suggesting columns; letters leaning against one another for support; and letters appearing in three-dimensions.

2 During another stage of the process, letterforms, lines, and shapes were combined into an image of an upraised hand symbolizing strength and trust.

3 Design investigations led to a logotype resembling a totem, which suggests the specialized products of Pillars. Shown are two color variations of the primary logotype. All of the letters in the word *pillars* are present in the configuration.

4–7 The logotype is capable of changing from one application to another just as the totems designed for Pillars' clients are capable of infinite variation. In spite of its changing nature, the logotype system is unified through a consistent use of type, color, and geometrical construction (see facing page and following spread).

pillars

p/llars

pillars

1

4

support

trust

2

3

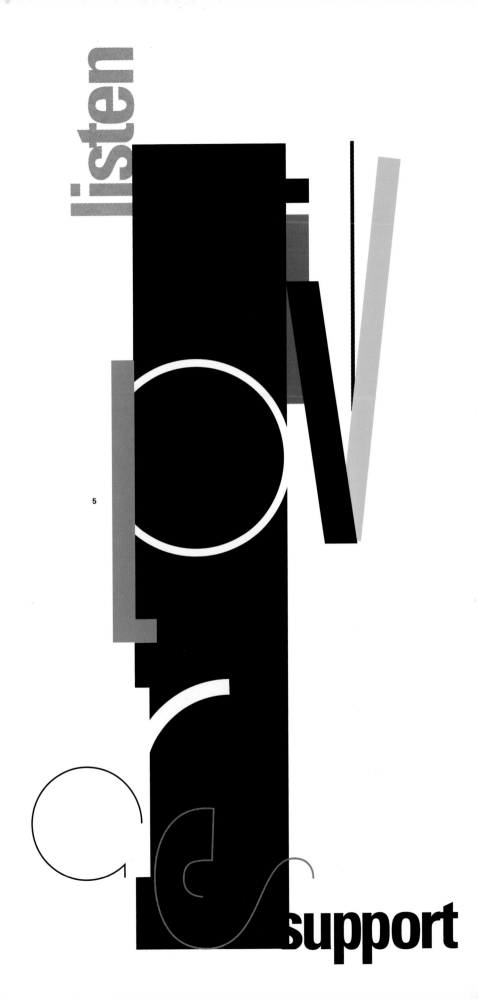

listen

support

5

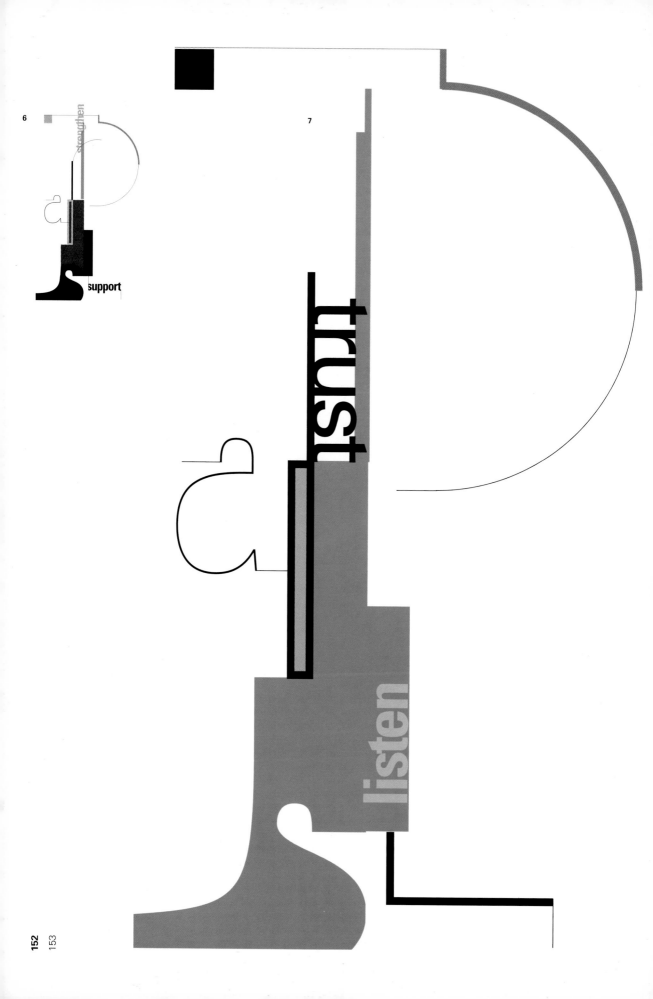

strengthen

support

trust

listen

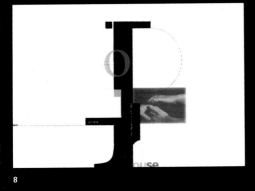

8

9

8-10 Identity applications include stationery, writing materials, invitations, and signage. Prototypes of actual totems reveal a lively conversation of form and color. These sculptural units contain drawers, sliding doors, and secret compartments for storing and preserving archival records and keepsakes.

10

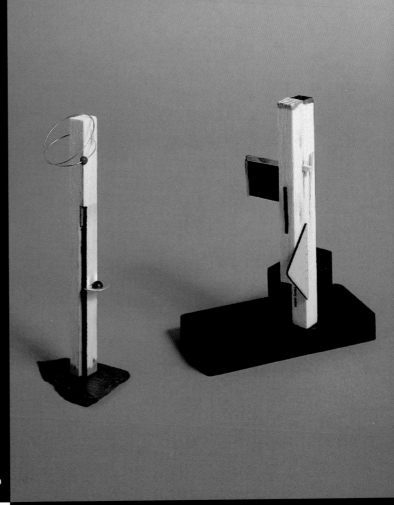

Alexander Isley Design
Alexander Isley
4 Old Mill Road
Redding, Connecticut 06896

Altitude
Alan Ball
48 Grove Street
Davis Square
Somerville, Massachusetts 02144

AND (Trafic Grafic)
Jean-Benoît Lévy
Spalenvorstadt 11
4051 Basel
Switzerland

Rob Carter
2920 Glendower Circle
Midlothian, Virginia 23113

Clarkson Creative
Larry G. Clarkson
1472 South 800 East
Salt Lake City, Utah 84107

David Colley
Communication Arts and Design
School of the Arts
Virginia Commonwealth
University
P.O. Box 842519
Richmond, Virginia 23284-2519

Communication Arts and Design
School of the Arts
Virginia Commonwealth
University
Ruth Baker
Jen Bracy
Lisa M. Helmstetter
Peter Martin
Nancy Nowacek
Amy A. Puglisi
Debbie Shmerler
P.O. Box 842519
Richmond, Virginia 23284-2519

Communication Design, Inc.
One North Fifth Street, Suite 500
Richmond, Virginia 23219

Crosby Associates Inc.
Bart Crosby
Tim Hartford
Angela Norwood
676 St. Clair
Chicago, Illinois 60611

5
John Malinoski
4204 Springhill Avenue
Richmond, Virginia 23225

Greimanski Labs
April Greiman
620 Moulton Avenue, # 211
Los Angeles, California 90031

Hutchinson Associates, Inc.
Jerry Hutchinson
1147 West Ohio, Suite 305
Chicago, Illinois 60622

Koeweiden Postma
W.G. Plein 516
Amsterdam, Netherlands

Lisa Levin Design
Lisa Levin
Jill Jacobson
124 Locust Avenue
Mill Valley, California 94941

Margo Chase Design
Margo Chase
2255 Bancroft Avenue
Los Angeles, California 90039

Meadows Design Office
Matt Woolman
4201 Connecticut Avenue NW
Suite 407
Washington, D.C. 20008

Minor Design Group
Cheryl Brzezinski-Beckett
1973 West Gray, Suite 22
Houston, Texas 77019

Morla Design
Jennifer Morla
Craig Bailey
463 Bryant Street
San Francisco, California 94107

Matsumoto Incorporated
Takaaki Matsumoto
220 West 19th Street
New York, New York 10011

Muller + Company
John Muller
4739 Belleview, Kansas City
Missouri 64112

Pentagram, Inc.
Paula Scher
204 Fifth Avenue
New York, New York 10010

Samenwerkende Ontwerpers
Iwan Daniëls
Mark Peters
Declan Stone
André Toet
Amsterdam, Netherlands

Segura Inc.
Carlos Segura
361 West Chestnut Street
First Floor
Chicago, Illinois 60610

David Shields
1411 North Wicker Park Avenue
Chicago, Illinois 60622

Siegel & Gale, Inc.
Raul Gutierrez
Elizabeth Burrill
3465 West Sixth Street
Suite 300
Los Angeles, California 90020

30sixty design
Brian Lane
Henry Vizcarra
2801 Cahuenga Blvd. West
Los Angeles, California 90068

TD2, S.C.
Rafael Treviño
Jose Luis Patiño
Nuevo León 270/404
Col. Condesa
06100 Mexico D.F.

Visser Bay Anders Toscani
Teun Anders
Ingeborg Bloem
Hilde Lohuis
Eric Nuyten
Assumburg 152, 1082 GC
Amsterdam, Netherlands

Adobe Systems, Incorporated
1585 Charleston Road
P.O. Box 7900
Mountain View, California
94039-7900

415 961 4400
800 64 ADOBE

Agfa Corporation
90 Industrial Way
Wilmington, Massachusetts 01887

508 658 5600

Autologic Inc.
1050 Rancho Conejo Blvd.
Thousand Oaks, California 91320

805 498 9611

H. Berthold AG
Teltowkanalstrasse 1–4
D-1000
Berlin 46, Germany

49 30 7795 439

Bitstream Inc.
Athenaeum House
215 First Street
Cambridge, Massachusetts 02142

800 237 3335

Carter & Cone Type, Inc.
2155 Massachusetts Avenue
Cambridge, Massachusetts 02140

1 617 876 5447
800 952 2129

Digital Typeface Corporation
9955 West 69th Street
Edden Prairie, Minnesota 55344

612 944 9264

Emigré
4475 D Street
Sacramento, California 95819

800 944 9021

FontHaus, Inc.
1375 Kings Highway East
Fairfield, Connecticut 06430

203 367 1993
800 942 9110

International Typeface Corporation (ITC)
866 Second Avenue
New York, New York 10017

212 371 0699

Linotype-Hell Company
425 Oser Avenue
Hauppauge, New York 11788

1 800 633 1900

Monotype Typography Inc.
Suite 2630
150 South Wacker Drive
Chicago, Illinois 60606

312 855 1440

[T-26]
361 West Chestnut Street
First Floor
Chicago, Illinois 60610

Varityper Inc.
11 Mount Pleasant Avenue
East Hanover, New Jersey 07936

800 526 0767

Items appearing in blue are concepts specifically related to working with computer type.

Typefaces are identified in *italics*.

Acknowledgements

Many thanks go to the contributing designers. Despite busy schedules, they kindly sent materials and provided information about their projects. I thank them for their countless E-mail messages and faxes; this book is about their excellent work. As always, my regarded colleagues, Philip Meggs and John Malinoski – with whom I work closely on a day to day basis – offered valuable advice and criticism. Diana Lively scrutinized the text and provided skilled copy editing. Mindy Carter once again compiled the index and offered much needed guidance. Amy Puglisi aided in the design of several spreads. Juggling hundreds of computer files from contributing designers, fixing software and system problems, and printing intermediate laser proofs would have been impossible without the knowledgeable guidance and help of Jerry Bates and Joseph Dimiceli. Thanks so much. I wish to extend warm thanks to my graduate students. Their enthusiasm for typographic design, and their hard work inspires my own process. At Virginia Commonwealth University, John DeMao offered support and encouragement. Sally Ann Carter, my wife, once again endured to the end, and did so while exhibiting patience and her special humor.

Working with Computer Type 2 was typeset and designed on a Power Macintosh 7100/66. Software used includes QuarkXPress, FreeHand, Illustrator, and PhotoShop. Text throughout the book is set in the Univers family.

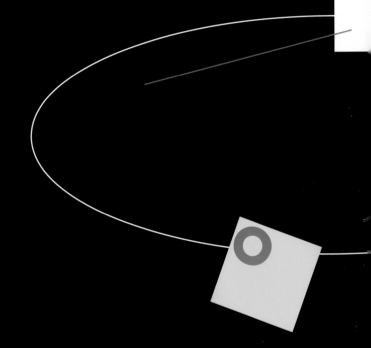

Identity